Effective Editing

Help Yourself in Becoming a Good Editor

Published by
Lotus Press

Effective Editing

Help Yourself in Becoming a Good Editor

Rashmi Sinha

4735/22, Prakash Deep Building,
Ansari Road, Daryaganj,
New Delhi- 110002

LOTUS PRESS Publishers & Distributors
Unit No. 220, Second Floor, 4735/22,
Prakash Deep Building, Ansari Road,
Daryaganj, New Delhi- 110002
Ph.: 32903912, 23280047, 098118-38000
E-mail: lotus_press@sify.com

Effective Editing

Help Yourself in Becoming Good Editor

ISBN 978-81-8382-268-8

Published by: **Lotus Press**, New Delhi.
Printed at: Concept Imprint, Delhi.

PREFACE

The word *Edit* is often cited as an example of back-formation. In other words, *Edit* is not the source of *Editor,* as *dive* is of *diver,* the expected derivational pattern; rather, the reverse is the case. *Edit* in the sense "to prepare for publication," first recorded in 1793, comes from *Editor,* first recorded in 1712 in the sense "one who Edits." There is more to the story, however.

Edit also comes partly from the French word *Editer,* "to publish, edit," first recorded in 1784. In the case of *Edit,* two processes, borrowing and back-formation, occurred either independently or together, perhaps one person originally taking *Edit* from French, another from *Editor,* and yet a third from both.

Editing can be defined as to prepare written material for publication or presentation, as by correcting, revising, or adapting.

It is the process of selecting and preparing language, images, sound, video, or film through processes of correction, condensation, organization, and other modifications in various media.

The word Editing is not limited to written material only, rather it's scope has really been widened now-a-days. Editing is an important part in many prominent fields, including printing and publishing, media, film industry etc.

This book is written keeping the ever growing importance of editing in mind and it covers editing for written material and covers some of the most important aspects of Editing including copyediting, proofreading, writing styles etc. We hope that this endeavour will be truly appreciated by all the readers and it will be useful for a wide range of readers.

Author

CONTENTS

Chapter 1

Editing: An Introduction

Editing is the process of selecting and preparing language, images, sound, video, or film through processes of correction, condensation, organization, and other modifications in various media. A person who edits is called an **editor.**

In a sense, the editing process originates with the idea for the work itself and continues in the relationship between the author and the editor.

Editing is, therefore, also a practice that includes creative skills, human relations, and a precise set of methods.

There are various editorial positions in publishing. Typically, one finds junior editorial assistants reporting to the senior-level editorial staff and directors who report to senior executive editors.

Senior executive editors are responsible for developing a product to its final release. The smaller the publication, the more these roles run together.

Copy editors correct spelling, grammar, and matters of

house style. At newspapers and wire services, they also write headlines and work on more-substantive issues, such as accuracy, fairness and taste. In some positions, they design pages and select of news stories for inclusion.

In European countries newspapers, the term is "sub-editor." They may choose the layout of the publication and communicate with the printer—a *production editor.*

This and similar jobs are also called "layout editor," "design editor," "news designer," or—more so in the past—"makeup editor."

Midlevel newspaper editors often manage or help manage sections, such as business, sports and features. In newspapers, the level below the top editor usually is the managing editor.

The title of the top editor at many publications may be called an "editor-in-chief," "executive editor" or just "editor."

Frequent and esteemed contributors to a magazine may acquire a title of *editor at-large* or *contributing editor*.

In the book publishing industry, editors organize anthologies and other compilations, produce definitive editions of a classic author's works ("scholarly editor"); and organize and manage contributions to a multi-author book (symposium editor or volume editor).

Finding marketable ideas and presenting them to appropriate authors are the responsibility of a sponsoring editor.

Obtaining copy or recruiting authors such as: an *acquisitions editor* or a *commissioning editor* for a publishing house.

Improving an author's writing so that they indeed say what they mean to say in an effective manner is substantive editing.

Depending on the writer's competence, this editing can sometimes turn into ghost writing.

Substantive editing is seldom a title. Many types of editors do this type of work, either in-house at a publisher or on an independent basis.

Changes to the publishing industry since the 1980s have resulted in nearly all copy editing of book manuscripts being outsourced to freelance copy editors.

Myths of Writing

1. Writing is for the transmission of information.

   Reality: While in the end the writing may convey information, it's major function is to explore ideas. The danger of the information-transmission myth is that it focuses on how texts are presented from the point of view of the reader rather than on what the act of writing can accomplish for the developing thought of the writer. The writer is overlooked.

2. Writing is for communication.

   Reality: The writer is always the First reader and may often be the only reader.

3. Writing involves transferring thoughts from the mind to paper.

   Reality: Thoughts are created in the act of writing, which changes the writer and changes the emerging text.

4. Writing is permanent.

Reality: Speech, once uttered, can rarely be revised; writing can be reflected upon, altered, and even erased at will.

5. Writing is a linear process.

   Reality: Writing can be done in several places and directions concurrently and is as easily manipulated in space as it is in time.

   Texts can be constructed from writing done on separate pieces of paper; words, sentences, paragraphs, whole sections can be shuffled into different sequences. Writing is recursive.

6. Writing is speech plus spelling and punctuation.

   Reality: Every kind of writing has its own conventions of form and expression quite different from speech.

   Spelling, punctuation, capitalization, paragraphing, indentation, word-dividing, layout, and so forth, are necessary aspects of transcription necessary to make written language readable for readers.

   For all writers, undue concern with transcription can interfere with the exploratory aspects of writing.

7. You must have something to say in order to write.

   Reality: We need to write in order to have anything to say! Thought comes with writing, and writing may never come if it is postponed until we are satisfied we have something to say. Write first, see what you had to say later.

8. Writing should be easy.

   Reality: Writing is often hard work—it requires concentration, physical effort, and a tolerance for frustration and disappointment.

9. Writing should be right the first time.

   Reality: Writing generally requires many drafts and revisions to get ideas into a form that satisfies the writer. A separate editorial polishing is required to make any text appropriate for another reader.

10. Writing should be unambiguous.

    Reality: There is no way writing can be unambiguous. "The" meaning of a text is not embedded in the words on the page but constructed by readers.

    The sense a reader constructs depends on what the reader knows and brings to the text. There is no way for any writer to know exactly what any reader brings to a text.

11. Writing can be done to order.

    Reality: Writing is most often reluctant to come when it is most urgently required, yet quite likely to begin to flow at inconvenient or impossible times.

12. A fixed period of "prewriting" should precede composing.

    Reality: Writing involves a lifetime of preparation—of experience, reading, reflecting and arguing. It is only from a transcription point of view that an author can say that work began on a particular text at a particular time. In fact, writing itself can be prewriting.

    As we draft one part of a text, we reflect on what we might write next or on what we have written already.

13. Writing is a solitary activity.

    Reality: Writing often requires other people to stimulate discussion, to listen to choice phrases, to provide feedback of various kinds.

14. Writing is a tidy activity.

    Reality: Writing is messy, it spreads itself all over the writing surface, in many different files.

15. Writing should be the same for everyone.

    Reality: Each of us develops an idiosyncratic set of strategies we're comfortable with and that work for us.

General tips for Editing

Focusing on the Reader

1. The Conventional Model

Writing as a two step process

- First—Figure out what you want to say
- Second—Put it into language

In essence this model looks like:

- Figure out what you want to say
- Don't start writing until you do
- Make a plan
- Use an outline
- Now begin writing

2. "The Five Step Writing Process"

- **Prewriting**—Organize your thoughts
- **Writing**—Prepare a draft
- **Revising**—Organizing the ideas in the draft
- **Editing**—Correcting grammar, spelling etc.
- **Publishing**—Developing a layout for the edited text

However this "communicating" model of writing is backwards.

- Instead of a two-step or five-step translation of meaning into language, writing is an organic, transactional process. You start writing at the very beginning—before you know your meaning at all.
- Only at the end will you know what you want to say and the words you want to use.
- You should expect to end up somewhere different from where you started—meaning is not what you start with but what you end up with.
- Think of writing not as a way to transmit a message but as a way of allowing your meaning to grow and evolve.
- Writing is a dynamic transaction with your thoughts, intentions, and words.

Writing from the Inside Out

Focusing on the Writer

1. Metaphor: Shaping at the Point of Utterance
   - **Preparation** – Reading, research, conversation, interviews
   - **Incubation** – The mulling around of ideas in the head
   - **Articulation** – The pen to paper phase of writing: drafting, amending, redrafting

Shaping at the Point of Utterance

- We focus on the end in view, shaping the utterance as we write; when a "seam is played out" or we are interrupted, we get started again by reading what we have written, running along tracks we have laid down.

- Writers develop an inner voice capable of "dictating" in the forms of written language.
- We cannot inspect the source of the words or the procedures by which they come; we just let them come, and they arrive—we can only decide whether or not we want to use the words we have generated after they arrive.
- We have no control at the instant of word production, but we have control before and after.

Notice in this metaphor "writing" involves a transaction between drafting, amending, redrafting and that incubation goes on throughout the entire process.

What we have is a description of the mental processes of the writer engaged in writing.

2. Metaphor: Writers Inside the Process
   - Writers aren't outside the process but an integral, interdependent part of it.
   - Writing is a process of transactions—
     - We enter into the act
     - We are changed during it, and
     - In turn we change our perceptions of the text being produced.

From this perspective, writing consists of ongoing writing episodes, based on both our global and focal intentions—our often vague inner sense of purpose, audience, possible form, and potential meaning.

In this metaphor there is dynamic interplay among reading, collecting, writing, connecting. It puts forth the idea that these activities occur in no particular order and each is affected by development in the others.

Writing Episodes

- A writing episode involves physically producing words on paper or screen; it's an extended act of "transacription" which results in a progressive development of a piece of text.
- Each writing act/episode influences our current thinking—what is written (or revised) becomes new information for us to reflect upon.
- Writing episodes occur intermittently, although our thought is continuous—sometimes words flow, one writing act/episode immediately following another; more usually there are pauses of varying length between episodes because our thought is reorganizing for forthcoming episodes or because of interruptions or distractions.
- Writing is a learning experience—we discover what we "mean" through the act of writing.

Specification of Intentions

- Intentions are the basis upon which a text is formed
- We have
    - **Global intentions**—Involving the purpose and overall form of a text.
    - **Focal intentions**—About the next word, phrase, sentence to be written.
- None of these intentions is part of the text itself; the text remains to be produced.

- These intentions are not a model of what the text will be like—many aspects of a text may be different from our original intentions.
- We often have no intentions for what a text will be like until particular parts of the text are actually produced.
- All the intentions represent the specification for the text:
    - The specification does not set out in detail what a text will be like.
    - The specification will be sketchy.
    - It includes some general expectations or intentions for what the finished text will be like.
- Some guidelines about its form:
    - Some parts of the specification may be quite detailed and specific (certain points will be covered in a certain order, even certain words or phrases that will be used).
    - In general, many details (whether something should be explained, how it should be explained) will be left until the actual moment of writing.
- The specification lays out the writer's "problem"—The emerging text is a solution to the problem if it meets our intentions and expectations.
- The specification is never complete, it often has many blanks.
- The specification must always be flexible; at no point will we know everything about what we are likely to write—
    - We may have general ideas about a particular paragraph, but we can't find the words or get the sentences ordered satisfactorily.

  - Sometimes words flow but take us in directions we don't intend.
  - We must let the words come because they are relevant to the general concerns although we don't know how to organize of constrain a particular paragraph.
- The specification is not an outline—It does not set out in detail the content and organization of a particular text; the specification for a text sets out the problems a writer has to solve in the process of writing.

The Transaction between Specification and Text

Composition is not simply a matter of translating a specification into words—The specification itself develops and changes as a text unfolds.

■■■

CHAPTER 2

Writing Process

About Writing

Writing is Creating Meaning

The wonderful thing about writing is that, contrary to popular belief, meaning is constructed as a result of writing not something worked out before you begin.

Writing isn't the transcription of pre-existent knowledge; every episode of writing requires an active construction of new meaning.

Purpose and Audience

You may not know the purpose of a particular piece of writing at the outset, although with most technical and business writing you usually have some general purpose as well as a specific or generic audience in mind. Whether you're writing an email or an in-depth technical report or proposal, at some point in the writing process you need to be able to articulate succinctly the purpose of a given piece of writing and you need to think about the assumptions you're making about your audience. As writing proceeds, both purpose and audience will become clearer; by the time you're done you should be able to say what it is you want your readers to understand.

Composing *vs* Revising/Editing

Composing is a constructing process; it's not transcribing thought that's already in your head.

When you begin, you may have only vague ideas about what you want to say—it's through writing that you sort out your thoughts, flesh them out, and organize them. Only after you've got a rough draft of your writing should you think about correctness: such things as spelling, punctuation, and grammar. That's why writing educators make a distinction between composing and editing—composing involves developing the material to make an argument or presentation; revising and editing are what you do once you have a rough version of what you want to say.

However, the act of writing really does combine all three aspects of the process. You will certainly find yourself revising as you go along—the important thing is to resist the temptation to make correctness your focus too early in the process.

Writing is Messy

Writing is a messy business.

I have notes to myself jotted on scraps of paper, on post-it notes, and on backs of envelopes. When I'm composing I keep paper handy so I can jot down ideas that I'm not sure I want to use or where I might use them. I have piles of reference material all over the desk and sometimes on the floor—I need that information handy so I can refer to something if I need to.

I write all over printouts of text; I save the mess because I never know if something I've thought of might be useful later. When I cut sections from a document, I paste them into an "out-takes" file so I won't regret having lost material.

There are false starts, and I get side-tracked but it's all part of the writing process. By the time I'm done, the document has been checked carefully for spelling, grammar and punctuation. It looks presentable; the mess is no longer visible. It's because the mess isn't visible in final versions that we forget that writing, of necessity, is a messy activity.

Invention Techniques

Initiating and Sustaining Composing

There are probably an infinite number of invention techniques; some popular ones are described below. Read about each one to see which works for you. Experiment and try to have some fun.

Freewriting

- Set a timer for five to ten minutes (you can always keep going after the beeper's gone off but an initial time limit is great for keeping you focused).
- Look at the topic and mull it over, roll it over your tongue, inhale it, let it bounce around the neural pathways of your brain for a second or two.
- Now ready? set? write! and don't stop! Keep your fingers typing or your pen moving on paper for the entire duration.
- Get it all out; a sort of intellectual diarrhea or stream-of-consciousness writing where you write what you think as you're thinking it.
- Don't worry about grammar, spelling, or forming

sentences. Some of it won't make sense and that's okay. If you find yourself drawing a blank at some point, then just write, "I'm drawing a blank" to keep the flow going or try and articulate why you think you can't get very far with the subject.

- There are no rules for this idea-generation technique except that
    1. You have to think (don't groan), and
    2. You can't censor yourself or read over what you've done until the timer has sounded (if you're doing this on a computer, a neat trick is to darken the screen to prevent this kind of senseless cheating).
- BZZZZTTTT! Time's up: now you can finally look over your stuff. Freewriting is great because sometimes you'll find you'll be able to lift off entire sections and use them in your first draft.

Brainstorming

This is quite similar to freewriting but the organization—the **way** you jot down ideas—is a bit different. Instead of an endless, non-punctuated, free-flowing paragraph, you only note down key words or short phrases on a page.

Set a timer, take a deep breath, and go crazy. If you get stuck, look at one of the ideas you've already written down and see if they don't trigger something new. Assume nothing is self-explanatory—at this stage stating the obvious is the best way to tap into original territory.

When you're done, use your word processor's cut and paste features (or arrows or color coding for you paper planners out there) to re-organize your terms and find relationships and common threads that might form subheadings.

Two ways to approach brainstorming:

(a) List Making

Here you simply jot down a stream of words or thoughts in a list format. There are no "wrong" thoughts to be had here. Try to limit the thoughts to a certain length. Also, try to commit to either a time or page goal—write three pages or write for five minutes, no more, no less.

(b) Diagramming

Great for people who work visually, diagramming can be a helpful way to provide structure to papers. Ignore the top to bottom, left to write motion of writing (or right to left, as the case may be) and simply write in a free fashion. Draw circles around your ideas, link them together using lines. Draw words in unusual shapes and liberally sprinkle your page with arrows, squares, question marks, and anything else you think might help represent your idea in a visual fashion.

The brainstorming process is about more than practicing writing, you should se e certain patterns and questions begin to emerge. Place your brainstorm writing aside for a while and then look at it later. You might be surprised at some of the things you've come up with. It's common for brainstorming and freewriting practitioners to wonder aloud, "Could I really have written that?"

Clustering/Webbing/Mapping

Basically the same as brainstorming but you start with a central word written in the middle of an unlined piece of paper. As related concepts pop in your head, you indicate them as branches, arrows, in bubbles, or however you like to cluster. Some branches will lead to dead ends, others will flourish. At the end of a successful cluster session, you'll focus on the blossoming areas and will even be able to draw arrows between concepts to show their relationships.

Again, no self-censorship allowed but don't beat a dead horse either. If one spark dies, return to the central or other provocative points you have scribbled in the lower right hand corner and try again.

Cubing

The general strategy of looking at your topic as you would a three-dimensional object with many sides. Sometimes you'll hear it called the "Many Parts Strategy" because it asks...no, pushes....you to consider your topic from a minimum of six different angles or avenues.

Heuristics

An impressive word that basically just means a learning aid or problem-solving technique that uses "self-education." Self-education is a bizarre but appropriate concept here because what you essentially do with any heuristic is interview yourself, tap into your own wealth of knowledge with the right drills in the right places, as it were. This is done by using questions as prompts.

One popular heuristic is the list of journalistic 5 Ws (and one H!): who, what, when, where, why, and how:

- What am I writing about? (topic)
- What am I trying to say about my topic? (controlling idea)
- Why am I writing about my topic? (purpose)
- Why should my reader(s) be interested in my controlling idea? (audience)
- What knowledge do I have that makes me the right person to write about this topic?

The Role of Talk in Writing

All of the above activities can be done orally with one or more colleagues—nowhere is it cast in stone that you have to sort out your ideas entirely on your own.

You can brainstorm or cluster/web/map with other people. Chart paper is helpful here, but you could use an electronic notebook to jot down ideas as they come up in discussion.

Sometimes, before attempting to capture your ideas in writing, it can be very useful to corner a colleague and say "Listen to me—" and quickly lay out what you're going to write about and how you might approach it. Having an audience quickly forces clarity.

Reading Like a Writer

Not sure how you want to tackle a particular writing task?

Try "Reading Like a Writer"—Find examples of the kind writing you're trying to do. Notice stylistic elements (tone of the writing, sentence variation, flow of ideas, formatting, etc....) and try reproducing them in your own writing as you write.

Finding Focus

Sometime you'll find you have a focus before you begin; other times your focus will emerge during the writing; sometimes you have to stand back and play with the emerging document to shape a focus.

Focusing Questions

- What's most important?
- What will my readers be looking for?

- What will my readers want to know more about?
- Can I identify a logical progression of ideas here?
- Might there be a better order for the content?
- Have I captured enough of the specifics?

Developing Focus

- Get yourself a set of colored highlighter pens.
- Work with a hard copy of your document.
- Take one pen, quickly read through your document, highlighting everything that seems to have some kind of common theme.
- Take a second pen, again quickly read through the document marking other paragraphs/sections that seem to have a different theme.
- Repeat a third and fourth time, if necessary.
- Now lay out your pages according to the predominant highlighting colour.
- Open your document file, "Save As" using a new file name—now cut all the information that's highlighted in other than the predominant colour (Be sure to paste this material into your out-takes file—you might well want it later!).
- Now read what you have – it will certainly be shorter, and it ought to have a definite focus.

Use A Reader: Ask For Feedback

- Have someone read what you've written—it's useful to tell him or her just what kind of feedback you're looking for. Another person often can see what you're driving at more easily than you can; you're too close to the writing.

Four Ways to Clarify

You have a draft—the next step is to make it clear, first to yourself and then to other readers.

It's important to remember you are your own first reader. You have to read your own copy to make sure it's clear to you, that you are saying what you want to say.

Now you must become a critical reader.

There are four main ways to clarify:

- **Discard**—You sense the writing doesn't work, it hasn't gone anywhere. Rather than belabour it, file the draft away and start again.
- **Reconceive**—You've got a first draft; now you need to go back and recollect, refocus and/or reorder. Because writing is recursive (that is, it keeps circling back on itself) you need to stand back and consider the meaning of the whole; do a quick read with an eye to other ways of "telling your story."
- **Rewrite**—There are two aspects of rewriting:
    - ***Revision***—Finding elements that require or warrant modification or elaboration in some way.
    - ***Editing***—Polishing the text to make it appropriate for readers.

Revision and Editing are Two Very Different Activities

With **revision,** you review the draft of a text from your own point of view to discover what the text contains. Respond to the text as if it were written by someone else. Only the writer can do revision because what matters is the effect of the text on the writer.

The aim of **editing** is not to change the text but to make what is there optimally readable. It is not necessary for a writer to do the editing; in fact, writers who publish typically are not responsible for final editing.

Editing is essentially a transcription skill. If you are editing yourself, you must try to respond to the text as a different reader.

The mistake most people make with editing is to plunge in and start editing the language of the text first, working from the written line back to form and then to meaning. That's got it backwards! You need to start with the overall meaning.

- ***Proof***—When you have done all reconceiving and revising you have time to do, then it's time to go through the text and eliminate superficial problems that will interfere with readers making meaning.

CHAPTER 3

Effective Writing

The Role of Introductions

Introductions and conclusions can be the most difficult parts of papers to write. Usually when you sit down to respond to an assignment, you have at least some sense of what you want to say in the body of your paper. You might have chosen a few examples you want to use or have an idea that will help you answer the question: these sections, therefore, are not as hard to write. But these middle parts of the paper can't just come out of thin air; they need to be introduced and concluded in a way that makes sense to your reader.

Your introduction and conclusion act as bridges that transport your readers from their own lives into the "place" of your analysis. If your readers pick up your paper about education in the autobiography of Mahatma Gandhi, for example, they need a transition to help them leave behind the world to help them temporarily enter the world of nineteenth-century freedom movement. By providing an introduction that helps your readers make a transition between their own world and the issues you will be writing about, you give your readers the tools they need to get into your topic and care about what you are saying.

Similarly, once you've hooked your reader with the introduction and offered evidence to prove your thesis, your conclusion can provide a bridge to help your readers make the transition back to their daily lives.

Why Bother Writing a Good Introduction?

1. **You never get a second chance to make a first impression**. The opening paragraph of your paper will provide your readers with their initial impressions of your argument, your writing style, and the overall quality of your work. A vague, disorganized, error-filled, off-the-wall, or boring introduction will probably create a negative impression.

   On the other hand, a concise, engaging, and well-written introduction will start your readers off thinking highly of you, your analytical skills, your writing, and your paper. This impression is especially important when the audience you are trying to reach (your instructor) will be grading your work.

2. **Your introduction is an important road map for the rest of your paper**. Your introduction conveys a lot of information to your readers. You can let them know what your topic is, why it is important, and how you plan to proceed with your discussion.

   It should contain a thesis that will assert your main argument. It will also, ideally, give the reader a sense of the kinds of information you will use to make that argument and the general organization of the paragraphs and pages that will follow. After reading your introduction, your readers should not have any major surprises in store when they read the main body of your paper.

3. **Ideally, your introduction will make your readers want to read your paper**. The introduction should capture your readers' interest, making them want to read the rest of your paper.

   Opening with a compelling story, a fascinating quotation, an interesting question, or a stirring example can get your readers to see why this topic matters and serve as an invitation for them to join you for an interesting intellectual conversation.

Strategies for Writing an Effective Introduction

- **Start by thinking about the question**. Your entire essay will be a response to the assigned question, and your introduction is the first step toward that end.

  Your direct answer to the assigned question will be your thesis, and your thesis will be included in your introduction, so it is a good idea to use the question as a jumping off point. Imagine that you are assigned the following question:

- Education has long been considered a major force for Indian social change, righting the wrongs of our society.

  Consider the following: What role did education play in the acquisition of freedom? Most importantly, consider the degree to which education was or was not a major force for social change with regard to independence.

- You will probably refer back to this question extensively as you prepare your complete essay, and the question itself can also give you some clues about how to approach the introduction.

Notice that the question starts with a broad statement, that education has been considered a major force for social change, and then narrows to focus on specific questions from the book. One strategy might be to use a similar model in your own introduction —start off with a big picture sentence or two about the power of education as a force for change as a way of getting your reader interested.

Of course, a different approach could also be very successful, but looking at the way the professor set up the question can sometimes give you some ideas for how you might answer it. Keep in mind, though, that even a "big picture" opening needs to be clearly related to your topic; an opening sentence that said "Human beings, more than any other creatures on earth, are capable of learning" would be too broad.

- **Try writing your introduction last**. You may think that you have to write your introduction first, but that isn't necessarily true, and it isn't always the most effective way to craft a good introduction.

  You may find that you don't know what you are going to argue at the beginning of the writing process, and only through the experience of writing your paper do you discover your main argument. It is perfectly fine to start out thinking that you want to argue a particular point, but wind up arguing something slightly or even dramatically different by the time you've written most of the paper. The writing process can be an important way to organize your ideas, think through complicated issues, refine your thoughts, and develop a sophisticated argument. However, an introduction written at the beginning of that discovery process will not necessarily reflect what you wind up with at the end.

You will need to revise your paper to make sure that the introduction, all of the evidence, and the conclusion reflect the argument you intend. Sometimes it helps to write up all of your evidence first and then write the introduction—that way you can be sure that the introduction matches the body of the paper.

- **Don't be afraid to write a tentative introduction first and then change it later.** Some people find that they need to write some kind of introduction in order to get the writing process started. That's fine, but if you are one of those people, be sure to return to your initial introduction later and rewrite if necessary.
- **Open with an attention grabber.** Sometimes, especially if the topic of your paper is somewhat dry or technical, opening with something catchy can help. Consider these options:
    - an intriguing example
    - a provocative quotation
    - a puzzling scenario
    - a vivid and perhaps unexpected anecdote
    - a thought-provoking question
- **Pay special attention to your first sentence**. Start off on the right foot with your readers by making sure that the first sentence actually says something useful and that it does so in an interesting and error-free way.
- **Be straightforward and confident**. Assert your main argument confidently. After all, you can't expect your reader to believe it if it doesn't sound like you believe it!

How to Evaluate your Introduction Draft?

Ask a friend to read it and then tell you what he or she expects the paper will discuss, what kinds of evidence the paper will use, and what the tone of the paper will be. If your friend is able to predict the rest of your paper accurately, you probably have a good introduction.

Five Kinds of Less Effective Introductions

1. **The place holder introduction**. When you don't have much to say on a given topic, it is easy to create this kind of introduction. Essentially, this kind of weaker introduction contains several sentences that are vague and don't really say much.

   They exist just to take up the "introduction space" in your paper. If you had something more effective to say, you would probably say it, but in the meantime this paragraph is just a place holder.

2. **The restated question introduction.** Restating the question can be an effective strategy, but it can be easy to stop at just restating the question instead of offering a more effective, interesting introduction to your paper. The professor or teaching assistant wrote your questions and will be reading ten to seventy essays in response to them—he or she does not need to read a whole paragraph that simply restates the question. Try to do something more interesting.

3. **The Webster's Dictionary introduction.** This introduction begins by giving the dictionary definition of one or more of the words in the assigned question. This introduction strategy is on the right track—if you write one of these, you may be trying to establish the important

terms of the discussion, and this move builds a bridge to the reader by offering a common, agreed-upon definition for a key idea.

You may also be looking for an authority that will lend credibility to your paper. However, anyone can look a word up in the dictionary and copy down what Webster says—it may be far more interesting for you (and your reader) if you develop your own definition of the term in the specific context of your class and assignment.

Also recognize that the dictionary is also not a particularly authoritative work—it doesn't take into account the context of your course and doesn't offer particularly detailed information. If you feel that you must seek out an authority, try to find one that is very relevant and specific. Perhaps a quotation from a source reading might prove better? Dictionary introductions are also ineffective simply because they are so overused. Many graders will see twenty or more papers that begin in this way, greatly decreasing the dramatic impact that any one of those papers will have.

4. **The "dawn of man" introduction.** This kind of introduction generally makes broad, sweeping statements about the relevance of this topic since the beginning of time.

   It is usually very general (similar to the place holder introduction) and fails to connect to the thesis. You may write this kind of introduction when you don't have much to say—which is precisely why it is ineffective.

5. **The book report introduction.** This introduction is what you had to do for your elementary school book reports. It

gives the name and author of the book you are writing about, tells what the book is about, and offers other basic facts about the book.

You might resort to this sort of introduction when you are trying to fill space because it's a familiar, comfortable format. It is ineffective because it offers details that your reader already knows and that are irrelevant to the thesis.

Conclusions

Introductions and conclusions can be the most difficult parts of papers to write. While the body is often easier to write, it needs a frame around it. An introduction and conclusion frame your thoughts and bridge your ideas for the reader.

Just as your introduction acts as a bridge that transports your readers from their own lives into the "place" of your analysis, your conclusion can provide a bridge to help your readers make the transition back to their daily lives. Such a conclusion will help them see why all your analysis and information should matter to them after they put the paper down.

Your conclusion is your chance to have the last word on the subject. The conclusion allows you to have the final say on the issues you have raised in your paper, to summarize your thoughts, to demonstrate the importance of your ideas, and to propel your reader to a new view of the subject. It is also your opportunity to make a good final impression and to end on a positive note.

Your conclusion can go beyond the confines of the assignment. The conclusion pushes beyond the boundaries of the prompt and allows you to consider broader issues, make new connections, and elaborate on the significance of your findings.

Your conclusion should make your readers glad that they read your paper. Your conclusion gives your reader something to take away that will help them see things differently or appreciate your topic in personally relevant ways. It can suggest broader implications that will not only interest your reader, but also enrich your reader's life in some way. It is your gift to the reader.

Strategies for Writing an Effective Conclusion

One or more of the following strategies may help you write an effective conclusion.

- Play the "So What" Game. If you're stuck and feel like your conclusion isn't saying anything new or interesting, ask a friend to read it with you. Whenever you make a statement from your conclusion, ask the friend to say, "So what?" or "Why should anybody care?" Then ponder that question and answer it. Here's how it might go:

  You: Basically, I'm just saying that education was important to Mr. M.K. Gandhi.

  Friend: *So what?*

  You: Well, it was important because it was a key to him feeling like a free and equal citizen.

  You can also use this strategy on your own, asking yourself "So What?" as you develop your ideas or your draft.

- Return to the theme or themes in the introduction. This strategy brings the reader full circle. For example, if you begin by describing a scenario, you can end with the same scenario as proof that your essay is helpful in creating a new understanding.

  You may also refer to the introductory paragraph by using

key words or parallel concepts and images that you also used in the introduction.

- Synthesize, don't summarize: Include a brief summary of the paper's main points, but don't simply repeat things that were in your paper.

  Instead, show your reader how the points you made and the support and examples you used fit together. Pull it all together.

- Include a provocative insight or quotation from the research or reading you did for your paper.
- Propose a course of action, a solution to an issue, or questions for further study. This can redirect your reader's thought process and help her to apply your info and ideas to her own life or to see the broader implications.
- Point to broader implications. For example, if your paper examines the event in the Civil Rights Movement, you could point out its impact on the Civil Rights Movement as a whole.

Strategies to Avoid

- Beginning with an unnecessary, overused phrase such as "in conclusion," "in summary," or "in closing." Although these phrases can work in speeches, they come across as wooden and trite in writing.
- Stating the thesis for the very first time in the conclusion.
- Introducing a new idea or subtopic in your conclusion.
- Ending with a rephrased thesis statement without any substantive changes.
- Making sentimental, emotional appeals that are out of character with the rest of an analytical paper.

- Including evidence (quotations, statistics, etc.) that should be in the body of the paper.

Four Kinds of Ineffective Conclusions

1. The "That's My Story and I'm Sticking to It" Conclusion. This conclusion just restates the thesis and is usually painfully short. It does not push the ideas forward. People write this kind of conclusion when they can't think of anything else to say.

2. The "Sherlock Holmes" Conclusion. Sometimes writers will state the thesis for the very first time in the conclusion. You might be tempted to use this strategy if you don't want to give everything away too early in your paper. You may think it would be more dramatic to keep the reader in the dark until the end and then "wow" him with your main idea, as in a Sherlock Holmes mystery.

   The reader, however, does not expect a mystery, but an analytical discussion of your topic in an academic style, with the main argument (thesis) stated up front. So, as the evidence demonstrates, Mahatma Gandhi saw education as a way to undermine the freedom fighters' power and also an important step toward freedom.

3. The "India the Beautiful"/"I Am Woman"/"We Shall Overcome" Conclusion. This kind of conclusion usually draws on emotion to make its appeal, but while this emotion and even sentimentality may be very heartfelt, it is usually out of character with the rest of an analytical paper. A more sophisticated commentary, rather than emotional praise, would be a more fitting tribute to the topic.

4. The "Grab Bag" Conclusion. This kind of conclusion includes extra information that the writer found or thought

of but couldn't integrate into the main paper. You may find it hard to leave out details that you discovered after hours of research and thought, but adding random facts and bits of evidence at the end of an otherwise-well-organized essay can just create confusion.

Thesis Statements

Writing in college often takes the form of persuasion—convincing others that you have an interesting, logical point of view on the subject you are studying. Persuasion is a skill you practice regularly in your daily life. You persuade your roommate to clean up, your parents to let you borrow the car, your friend to vote for your favorite candidate or policy. In college, course assignments often ask you to make a persuasive case in writing. You are asked to convince your reader of your point of view.

This form of persuasion, often called academic argument, follows a predictable pattern in writing. After a brief introduction of your topic, you state your point of view on the topic directly and often in one sentence. This sentence is the thesis statement, and it serves as a summary of the argument you'll make in the rest of your paper.

What is a Thesis Statement?

A Thesis Statement:

- tells the reader how you will interpret the significance of the subject matter under discussion.
- is a road map for the paper; in other words, it tells the reader what to expect from the rest of the paper.
- directly answers the question asked of you. A thesis is an interpretation of a question or subject, not the subject itself.

The subject, or topic, of an essay might be World War II a thesis must then offer a way to understand the war.

- makes a claim that others might dispute.
- is usually a single sentence somewhere in your first paragraph that presents your argument to the reader. The rest of the paper, the body of the essay, gathers and organizes evidence that will persuade the reader of the logic of your interpretation.

If your assignment asks you to take a position or develop a claim about a subject, you may need to convey that position or claim in a thesis statement near the beginning of your draft. The assignment may not explicitly state that you need a thesis statement because your instructor may assume you will include one.

When in doubt, ask your instructor if the assignment requires a thesis statement. When an assignment asks you to analyze, to interpret, to compare and contrast, to demonstrate cause and effect, or to take a stand on an issue, it is likely that you are being asked to develop a thesis and to support it persuasively.

How do I get a Thesis?

A thesis is the result of a lengthy thinking process. Formulating a thesis is not the first thing you do after reading an essay assignment. Before you develop an argument on any topic, you have to collect and organize evidence, look for possible relationships between known facts (such as surprising contrasts or similarities), and think about the significance of these relationships.

Once you do this thinking, you will probably have a "working thesis," a basic or main idea, an argument that you think you can support with evidence but that may need adjustment along the way.

Writers use all kinds of techniques to stimulate their thinking and to help them clarify relationships or comprehend the broader significance of a topic and arrive at a thesis statement.

How do I know if my Thesis is Strong?

If there's time, run it by your instructor or make an appointment at the Writing Centre to get some feedback. Even if you do not have time to get advice elsewhere, you can do some thesis evaluation of your own. When reviewing your first draft and its working thesis, ask yourself the following:

- *Do I answer the question?* Re-reading the question prompt after constructing a working thesis can help you fix an argument that misses the focus of the question.
- *Have I taken a position that others might challenge or oppose?*If your thesis simply states facts that no one would, or even could, disagree with, it's possible that you are simply providing a summary, rather than making an argument.
- Is my thesis statement specific enough?

Thesis statements that are too vague often do not have a strong argument. If your thesis contains words like "good" or "successful," see if you could be more specific: *why* is something "good"; *what specifically* makes something "successful"?

- *Does my thesis pass the "So what?" test?* If a reader's first response is, "So what?" then you need to clarify, to forge a relationship, or to connect to a larger issue.
- *Does my essay support my thesis specifically and without wandering?* If your thesis and the body of your essay do

not seem to go together, one of them has to change. It's o.k. to change your working thesis to reflect things you have figured out in the course of writing your paper. Remember, always reassess and revise your writing as necessary.

- *Does my thesis pass the "how and why?" test?* If a reader's first response is "how?" or "why?" your thesis may be too open-ended and lack guidance for the reader. See what you can add to give the reader a better take on your position right from the beginning.

Transitions

The Function and Importance of Transitions

In both academic writing and professional writing, your goal is to convey information clearly and concisely, if not to convert the reader to your way of thinking. Transitions help you to achieve these goals by establishing logical connections between sentences, paragraphs, and sections of your papers. In other words, transitions tell readers what to do with the information you present them.

Whether single words, quick phrases or full sentences, they function as signs for readers that tell them how to think about, organize, and react to old and new ideas as they read through what you have written.

Transitions signal relationships between ideas such as: "Another example coming up—stay alert!" or "Here's an exception to my previous statement" or "Although this idea appears to be true, here's the real story."

Basically, transitions provide the reader with directions for how to piece together your ideas into a logically coherent argument.

Transitions are not just verbal decorations that embellish your paper by making it sound or read better. They are words with particular meanings that tell the reader to think and react in a particular way to your ideas. In providing the reader with these important cues, transitions help readers understand the logic of how your ideas fit together.

Signs that you might need to Work on your Transitions

How can you tell whether you need to work on your transitions? Here are some possible clues:

- Your instructor has written comments like "choppy," "jumpy," "abrupt," "flow," "need signposts," or "how is this related?" on your papers.
- Your readers (instructors, friends, or classmates) tell you that they had trouble following your organization or train of thought.
- You tend to write the way you think—and your brain often jumps from one idea to another pretty quickly.
- You wrote your paper in several discrete "chunks" and then pasted them together.
- You are working on a group paper; the draft you are working on was created by pasting pieces of several people's writing together.

Organization

Since the clarity and effectiveness of your transitions will depend greatly on how well you have organized your paper, you may want to evaluate your paper's organization before you work on transitions. In the margins of your draft, summarize in a word or short phrase what each paragraph is about or how it fits into your analysis as a whole. This exercise should help you to see the order of and connection between your ideas more clearly.

How Transitions Work?

The organization of your written work includes two elements:

1. The order in which you have chosen to present the different parts of your discussion or argument, and
2. The relationships you construct between these parts. Transitions cannot substitute for good organization, but they can make your organization clearer and easier to follow. Take a look at the following example:

A hypothetical country for example "C", has a new democratic government after having been a dictatorship for many years. Assume that you want to argue that C is not as democratic as the conventional view would have us believe. One way to effectively organize your argument would be to present the conventional view and then to provide the reader with your critical response to this view. So, in argument A you would enumerate all the reasons that someone might consider C highly democratic, while in argument B you would refute these points. The transition that would establish the logical connection between these two key elements of your argument would indicate to the reader that the information in paragraph B contradicts the information in paragraph A. As a result, you might organize your argument, including the transition that links paragraph A with paragraph B, in the following manner:

Argument A: Points that support the view that C's new government is very democratic.

Transition: Despite the previous arguments, there are

many reasons to think that C's new government is not as democratic as typically believed.

Argument B: Points that contradict the view that C's new government is very democratic.

In this case, the transition words "Despite the previous arguments," suggest that the reader should not believe paragraph A and instead should consider the writer's reasons for viewing C's democracy as suspect.

As the example suggests, transitions can help reinforce the underlying logic of your paper's organization by providing the reader with essential information regarding the relationship between your ideas.

In this way, transitions act as the glue that binds the components of your argument or discussion into a unified, coherent, and persuasive whole.

Types of Transitions

Now that you have a general idea of how to go about developing effective transitions in your writing, let us briefly discuss the types of transitions your writing will use.

The types of transitions available to you are as diverse as the circumstances in which you need to use them. A transition can be a single word, a phrase, a sentence, or an entire paragraph. In each case, it functions the same way: first, the transition either directly summarizes the content of a preceding sentence, paragraph, or section, or it implies that summary. Then it helps the reader anticipate or comprehend the new information that you wish to present.

1. **Transitions between sections**—Particularly in longer works, it may be necessary to include transitional paragraphs that summarize for the reader the information

just covered and specify the relevance of this information to the discussion in the following section.

2. **Transitions between paragraphs**—If you have done a good job of arranging paragraphs so that the content of one leads logically to the next, the transition will highlight a relationship that already exists by summarizing the previous paragraph and suggesting something of the content of the paragraph that follows.

   A transition between paragraphs can be a word or two (*however, for example, similarly*), a phrase, or a sentence. Transitions can be at the end of the first paragraph, at the beginning of the second paragraph, or in both places.

3. **Transitions within paragraphs**—As with transitions between sections and paragraphs, transitions within paragraphs act as cues by helping readers to anticipate what is coming before they read it. Within paragraphs, transitions tend to be single words or short phrases.

Paragraph Development

Paragraphs are the building blocks of papers. Many students define paragraphs in terms of length: a paragraph is a group of at least five sentences, a paragraph is half a page long, etc. In reality, though, the unity and coherence of ideas among sentences is what constitutes a paragraph.

A paragraph is defined as "a group of sentences or a single sentence that forms a unit". Length and appearance do not determine whether a section in a paper is a paragraph. For instance, in some styles of writing, particularly journalistic styles, a paragraph can be just one sentence long.

Ultimately, a paragraph is a sentence or group of sentences

that support one main idea. In this analysis, we will refer to this as the "controlling idea," because it controls what happens in the rest of the paragraph.

How do I Decide What to Put in a Paragraph?

Before you can begin to determine what the composition of a particular paragraph will be, you must first decide on a working thesis for your paper. What is the most important idea that you are trying to convey to your reader? The information in each paragraph must be related to that idea.

In other words, your paragraphs should remind your reader that there is a recurrent relationship between your thesis and the information in each paragraph. A working thesis functions like a seed from which your paper, and your ideas, will grow. The whole process is an organic one—a natural progression from a seed to a full-blown paper where there are direct, familial relationships between all of the ideas in the paper.

The decision about what to put into your paragraphs begins with the germination of a seed of ideas; this "germination process" is better known as brainstorming. There are many techniques for brainstorming; whichever one you choose, this stage of paragraph development cannot be skipped. Building paragraphs can be like building a skyscraper: there must be a well-planned foundation that supports what you are building. Any cracks, inconsistencies, or other corruptions of the foundation can cause your whole paper to crumble.

So, let's suppose that you have done some brainstorming to develop your thesis. What else should you keep in mind as you begin to create paragraphs? Every paragraph in a paper should be.

- **Unified**—All of the sentences in a single paragraph should be related to a single controlling idea (often expressed in the topic sentence of the paragraph).
- **Clearly related to the thesis**—The sentences should all refer to the central idea, or thesis, of the paper.
- **Coherent**—The sentences should be arranged in a logical manner and should follow a definite plan for development.
- **Well-developed**—Every idea discussed in the paragraph should be adequately explained and supported through evidence and details that work together to explain the paragraph's controlling idea.

How do I Organize a Paragraph?

There are many different ways to organize a paragraph. The organization you choose will depend on the controlling idea of the paragraph. Below are a few possibilities for organization, with brief examples.

Example:

Narration: Tell a story. Go chronologically, from start to finish.

One man found quite a surprise last year while fishing in the River: a Piranha. He reeled in a one pound, four ounce fish with an unusual bite. He could not identify it, but a nearby fisherman did. He at first could not believe he had caught a piranha.

He said, "That ain't no piranha. They ain't got piranha around here." He was right: the fish is native to South America, and North Carolina prohibits owning the fish as a pet or introducing the species to local waterways. The sharp-toothed, carnivorous fish likely found itself in the river when its illegal owner released the fish after growing tired of it. Wildlife officials hope that the piranha was the only of its kind in the river, but locals are thinking twice before they wade in the water.

Description: Provide specific details about what something looks, smells, tastes, sounds, or feels like. Organize spatially, in order of appearance, or by topic.

Piranha are omnivorous, freshwater fish, which are mostly known for their single row of sharp, triangular teeth in both jaws. Piranhas' teeth come together in a scissor-like bite and are used for puncture and tearing.

Baby piranha are small, about the size of a thumbnail, but full-grown piranha grow up to about 6-10 inches, and some individual fish up to 2 feet long have been found. The many species of piranha vary in color, though most are either silvery with an orange underbelly and throat or almost entirely black.

Process: Explain how something works, step by step. Perhaps follow a sequence—first, second, third.

You can safely swim with piranhas, but it's important to know how and when to do it. First, chose an appropriate time, preferably at night and during the rainy season. Avoid piranha-infested waters during the dry season, when food supplies are low and piranhas are more desperate.

Piranhas feed during the day, so night-time swimming is much safer. Second, streamline your movement. Wild or erratic activity attracts the attention of piranhas. Swim slowly and smoothly.

Finally, never enter the water with an open wound or raw meat. Piranhas attack larger animals only when they are wounded. The presence of blood in the water may tempt the fish to attack. If you follow these simple precautions, you will have little to fear.

Classification: Separate into groups or explain the various parts of a topic.

Piranhas comprise more than 30-60 species of fish, depending on whom you ask. The many species fall into four genera: Pygocentrus, Pygopristis, Serrasalmus, and Pristobrycon.

Piranha in the Pygocentrus genus are the most common variety, the kind you might find in a pet store. Pygopristis piranha are herbivores, feasting on seeds and fruits, not flesh. In contrast, fish in the Serrasalmus genus eat only meat, and their teeth are razor-sharp. Pristobrycon are the least friendly of all piranhas; they often bite the fins of other fish, even fish of the same species. The label piranha, then, refers to a wide variety of species.

5-step Process to Paragraph Development

Let's walk through a 5-step process to building a paragraph. Each step of the process will include an explanation of the step and a bit of "model" text to illustrate how the step works.

Our finished model paragraph will be about slave spirituals, the original songs that African Americans created during slavery. The model paragraph uses illustration (giving examples) to prove its point.

Step 1. Decide on a Controlling Idea and Create a Topic Sentence

Paragraph development begins with the formulation of the controlling idea. This idea directs the paragraph's development. Often, the controlling idea of a paragraph will appear in the form of a topic sentence.

In some cases, you may need more than one sentence to express a paragraph's controlling idea.

Step 2. Explain the Controlling Idea

- Paragraph development continues with an expression of the rationale or the explanation that the writer gives for how the reader should interpret the information presented in the idea statement or topic sentence of the paragraph.

  The writer explains his/her thinking about the main topic, idea, or focus of the paragraph. Here's the sentence that would follow the controlling idea about slave spirituals:

Model Explanation—On one level, spirituals referenced heaven, Jesus, and the soul; but on another level, the songs spoke about slave resistance.

Step 3. Give an Example (or Multiple Examples)

- Paragraph development progresses with the expression of some type of support or evidence for the idea and the explanation that came before it. The example serves as a sign or representation of the relationship established in the idea and explanation portions of the paragraph. Here are two examples that we could use to illustrate the double meanings in slave spirituals:

Model Example A— According to Frederick Douglass, the song "O Canaan, Sweet Canaan" spoke of slaves' longing for heaven, but it also expressed their desire to escape to the North. Careful listeners heard this second meaning in the following lyrics: "I don't expect to stay / Much longer here. Run to Jesus, shun the danger. / I don't expect to stay."

Model Example B— Slaves even used songs like "Steal Away to Jesus (at midnight)" to announce to other slaves the time and place of secret, forbidden meetings.

Step 4. Explain the Example(s)

The next movement in paragraph development is an explanation of each example and its relevance to the topic sentence and rationale that were stated at the beginning of the paragraph. This explanation shows readers why you chose to use this/or these particular examples as evidence to support the major claim, or focus, in your paragraph.

Continue the pattern of giving examples and explaining them until all points/examples that the writer deems necessary have been made and explained. None of your examples should be left unexplained. You might be able to explain the relationship between the example and the topic sentence in the same sentence which introduced the example.

More often, however, you will need to explain that relationship in a separate sentence. Look at these explanations for the two examples in the slave spirituals paragraph:

Model Explanation for Example A— When slaves sang this song, they could have been speaking of their departure from this life and their arrival in heaven; however, they also could have been describing their plans to leave the South and run, not to Jesus, but to the North.

Model Explanation for Example B—[The relationship between example B and the main idea of the paragraph's controlling idea is clear enough without adding another sentence to explain it.]

Step 5. Complete the Paragraph's Idea or Transition into the Next Paragraph

The final movement in paragraph development involves tying

up the loose ends of the paragraph and reminding the reader of the relevance of the information in this paragraph to the main or controlling idea of the paper.

At this point, you can remind your reader about the relevance of the information that you just discussed in the paragraph.

You might feel more comfortable, however, simply transitioning your reader to the next development in the next paragraph. Here's an example of a sentence that completes the slave spirituals paragraph:

Model Sentence for Completing a Paragraph— What whites heard as merely spiritual songs, slaves discerned as detailed messages. The hidden meanings in spirituals allowed slaves to sing what they could not say.

An Example of Completed "Model" Paragraph

Slave spirituals often had hidden double meanings. On one level, spirituals referenced heaven, Jesus, and the soul, but on another level, the songs spoke about slave resistance.

For example, according to Frederick Douglass, the song "O Canaan, Sweet Canaan" spoke of slaves' longing for heaven, but it also expressed their desire to escape to the North.

Careful listeners heard this second meaning in the following lyrics: "I don't expect to stay / Much longer here. / Run to Jesus, shun the danger. / I don't expect to stay." When slaves sang this song, they could have been speaking of their departure from this life and their arrival in heaven; however, they also could have been describing their plans to leave the South and run, not to Jesus, but to the North. Slaves even used songs like "Steal Away to Jesus (at midnight)" to announce to other slaves the time and place of secret, forbidden meetings. What whites heard as merely spiritual songs, slaves discerned as detailed messages. The hidden meanings in spirituals allowed slaves to sing what they could not say.

Troubleshooting Paragraphs

1. **Problem: The paragraph has no topic sentence.** Imagine each paragraph as a sandwich. The real content of the sandwich—the meat or other filling—is in the middle. In includes all the evidence you need to make the point. But it gets kind of messy to eat a sandwich without any bread. Your readers don't know what to do with all the evidence you've given them.

   So, the top slice of bread (the first sentence of the paragraph) explains the topic (or controlling idea) of the paragraph. And, the bottom slice (the last sentence of the paragraph) tells the reader how the paragraph relates to the broader argument. In the original and revised paragraphs below, notice how a topic sentence expressing the controlling idea tells the reader the point of all the evidence.

Original Paragraph

Piranhas rarely feed on large animals; they eat smaller fish and aquatic plants. When confronted with humans, piranhas' first instinct is to flee, not attack. Their fear of humans makes sense. Far more piranhas are eaten by people than people are eaten by piranhas. If the fish are well-fed, they won't bite humans.

Revised Paragraph

Although most people consider piranhas to be quite dangerous, they are, for the most part, entirely harmless. Piranhas rarely feed on large animals; they eat smaller fish and aquatic plants.

When confronted with humans, piranhas' first instinct is to flee, not attack. Their fear of humans makes sense. Far more piranhas are eaten by people than people are eaten by piranhas. If the fish are well-fed, they won't bite humans.

Once you have mastered the use of topic sentences, you may decide that the topic sentence for a particular paragraph really shouldn't be the first sentence of the paragraph. This is fine—the topic sentence can actually go at the beginning, middle, or end of a paragraph; what's important is that it is in there somewhere so that readers know what the main idea of the paragraph is and how it relates back to the thesis of your paper.

Suppose that we wanted to start the piranha paragraph with a transition sentence—something that reminds the reader of what happened in the previous paragraph—rather than with the topic sentence. Let's suppose that the previous paragraph was about all kinds of animals that people are afraid of, like sharks, snakes, and spiders. Our paragraph might look like this (the topic sentence is underlined):

Like sharks, snakes, and spiders, pirahnas are widely feared. Although most people consider piranhas to be quite dangerous, they are, for the most part, entirely harmless. Piranhas rarely feed on large animals; they eat smaller fish and aquatic plants.

When confronted with humans, piranhas' first instinct is to flee, not attack. Their fear of humans makes sense. Far more piranhas are eaten by people than people are eaten by piranhas. If the fish are well-fed, they won't bite humans.

2. **Problem: the paragraph has more than one controlling idea.** If a paragraph has more than one main idea, consider eliminating sentences that relate to the second idea, or split

the paragraph into two or more paragraphs, each with only one main idea.

In the following paragraph, the final two sentences branch off into a different topic; so, the revised paragraph eliminates them and concludes with a sentence that reminds the reader of the paragraph's main idea.

Original Paragraph

Although most people consider piranhas to be quite dangerous, they are, for the most part, entirely harmless. Piranhas rarely feed on large animals; they eat smaller fish and aquatic plants. When confronted with humans, piranhas' first instinct is to flee, not attack. Their fear of humans makes sense. Far more piranhas are eaten by people than people are eaten by piranhas.

Revised paragraph

Although most people consider piranhas to be quite dangerous, they are, for the most part, entirely harmless. Piranhas rarely feed on large animals; they eat smaller fish and aquatic plants.

When confronted with humans, piranhas' first instinct is to flee, not attack. Their fear of humans makes sense. Far more piranhas are eaten by people than people are eaten by piranhas.

3. **Problem: transitions are needed within the paragraph.** You are probably familiar with the idea that transitions may be needed between paragraphs or sections in a paper. Sometimes they are also helpful within the body of a single paragraph.

   Within a paragraph, transitions are often single words or short phrases that help to establish relationships between ideas and to create a logical progression of those ideas in a paragraph. This is especially likely to be true within paragraphs that discuss multiple examples. Let's take a look at a version of our piranha paragraph that uses transitions to orient the reader:

Although most people consider piranhas to be quite dangerous, they are, except in two main situations, entirely harmless. Piranhas rarely feed on large animals; they eat smaller fish and aquatic plants.

When confronted with humans, piranhas' instinct is to flee, not attack. But there are two situations in which a piranha bite is likely. The first is when a frightened piranha is lifted out of the water—for example, if it has been caught in a fishing net. The second is when the water level in pools where piranhas are living falls too low. A large number of fish may be trapped in a single pool, and if they are hungry, they may attack anything that enters the water.

In this example, you can see how the phrases "the first" and "the second" help the reader follow the organization of the ideas in the paragraph.

Gender-Sensitive Language

English speakers and writers have traditionally been taught to use masculine nouns and pronouns in situations where the gender of their subject(s) is unclear or variable, or when a group to which they are referring contains members of both sexes.

For example, the US Declaration of Independence states that " . . . all men are created equal . . ." and most of us were taught in elementary school to understand the word "men" in that context includes both male and female.

In recent decades, however, as women have become

increasingly involved in the public sphere of life, writers have reconsidered the way they express gender identities and relationships.

Because most English language readers no longer understand the word "man" to be synonymous with "people," writers today must think more carefully about the ways they express gender in order to convey their ideas clearly and accurately to their readers.

Moreover, these issues are important for people concerned about issues of social inequality. There is a relationship between our language use and our social reality. If we "erase" women from language, that makes it easier to maintain gender inequality.

As Professor Sherryl Kleinman has argued, [M]ale-based generics are another indicator—and, more importantly, a *reinforcer*—of a system in which "man" in the abstract and men in the flesh are privileged over women.

Words matter, and our language choices have consequences. If we believe that women and men deserve social equality, then we should think seriously about how to reflect that belief in our language use.

If you're reading this analysis, you're probably already aware that tackling gender sensitivity in your writing is no small task, especially since there isn't yet (and there may never be) a set of concrete guidelines on which to base your decisions. Fortunately, there are a number of different strategies the gender-savvy writer can use to express gender relationships with precision. This analysis will provide you with an overview of some of those strategies so that you can "mix and match" as necessary when you write.

Pronouns

A pronoun is a word that substitutes for a noun. The English language provides pronoun options for references to masculine nouns (for example, "he" can substitute for "Titoo"), feminine nouns ("she" can replace "Priyanka"), and neutral/non-human nouns ("it" stands in for "a tree"), but no choice for sex-neutral third-person singular nouns ("the writer," "a student," or "someone").

Although most of us learned in elementary school that masculine pronouns (he, his, him) should be used as the "default" in situations where the referent (that is, the person or thing to which you're referring) could be either male or female, that usage is generally considered unacceptable now. So what should you do when you're faced with one of those gender-neutral or gender-ambiguous situations? Well, you've got a few options . . .

1. Use "they"

This option is currently much debated by grammar experts, but most agree that it works well in at least several kinds of situations. In order to use "they" to express accurately gender relationships, you'll need to understand that "they" is traditionally used only to refer to a plural noun. For example:

Sojourner Truth and Elizabeth Cady Stanton were famous "first-wave" American feminists. They were also both involved in the Abolitionist movement.

In speech, though, we early twenty-first century we commonly use "they" to refer to a singular referent. According to many grammar experts, that usage is incorrect, but here's an example of how it sounds in our everyday speech:

If **a student** wants to learn more about gender inequality,

they should take Intro to Women's Studies. Note that in this example, "a student" is singular, but it is replaced in the second sentence by "they," a plural pronoun. In speech, we often don't notice such substitutions of the plural for the singular, but in writing, some will find such substitutions awkward or incorrect.

Some people argue that "they" should become the default gender-neutral pronoun for English writing, but since that usage can still sound awkward to many readers, its best to use "they" only in plural situations.

Thus, one other option the gender-savvy writer may choose to employ is to make her/his sentence plural. Here's one way that can work:

A student's beliefs about feminism may be based on what **he** has heard in the popular media.

Students' beliefs about feminism may be based on what **they** have heard in the popular media.

2. Use She or He or She/He

Another, simpler option the gender-savvy writer can use to deal with situations in which the gender of the referent is unknown or variable is to write out both pronoun options as "she or he" or "she/he". For example:

Each **student** who majors in Women's Studies major must take a course in Feminist Theory.

She or he may also get course credit for completing an internship at a local organization that benefits women.

OR

Each **student** who majors in Women's Studies major must take a course in Feminist Theory. **She/he** may also get course credit for completing an internship at a local organization that benefits women.

3. Alternate Genders and Pronouns

You may also choose to alternate gendered pronouns. This option will work only in certain situations, though—usually hypothetical situations in which the referent is equally likely to be a male or a female.

For example, both male and female students use the Writing Center's services, so the author of our staff manual chose to alternate between masculine and feminine pronouns when writing the following tutoring guidelines:

- Respond as a reader, explaining what and how you were/are thinking as you read her texts so that she can discover where a reader might struggle with her writing.
- Ask him to outline the draft to reveal the organization of the paper.
- Ask her to describe her purpose and audience and show how she has taken them into account in her writing.
- Explain a recurring pattern and let him locate repeated instances of it.

Of course, we could also have included both pronouns in each sentence by writing "her/his" or "her/him," but in this case, alternating "he" and "she" conveys the same sense of gender variability and is likely a little easier on the reader, who won't have to pause to process several different options every time a gendered pronoun is needed in the sentence.

This example also provides a useful demonstration of how gender-savvy writers can take advantage of the many different options available by choosing the one that best suits the unique requirements of each piece of writing they produce.

4. Eliminate the Pronoun Altogether

Finally, you can also simply eliminate the pronoun. For example,

Allan Johnson is a contemporary feminist theorist. This **writer and professor** gave a speech at UNC in the fall of 2007.

Note how the sentence used "this writer and professor" rather than "he."

Many people accept the negative stereotype that if a person is a feminist, **she** must hate men.

Many people accept the negative stereotype that **feminist beliefs** are based on hatred of men.

Note how the second version of the sentence talks about the beliefs. By avoiding using the pronoun "she," it leaves open the possibility that men may be feminists.

Gendered Nouns

Like gendered pronouns, gendered nouns can also provide a stumbling block for the gender-savvy writer. The best way to avoid implications these words can carry is simply to be aware of how we tend to use them in speech and writing.

Because gendered nouns are so commonly used and accepted by English writers and speakers, we often don't notice them or the implications they bring with them.

Once you've recognized that a gender distinction is being made by such a word, though, conversion of the gendered noun into a gender-savvy one is usually very simple.

"Man" and words ending in "-man" are the most commonly used gendered nouns, so avoiding the confusion they bring can be as simple as watching out for these words and replacing them with words that convey your meaning more effectively.

For example, if some ancient writers were gender-savvy, they might have written " . . . all people are created equal" instead of " . . . all men are created equal . ..."

Another common gendered expression, particularly in informal speech and writing, is "you guys." This expression is used to refer to groups of men, groups of women, and groups that include both men and women.

Although most people *mean* to be inclusive when they use "you guys," this phrase wouldn't make sense if it didn't subsume women under the category "guys." To see why "you guys" is gendered male, consider that "a guy" (singular) is definitely a man, not a woman, and that most men would not feel included in the expression "you gals" or "you girls."

Another example of gendered language is the way the words "Mr.," "Miss," and "Mrs." are used. "Mr." can refer to any man, regardless of whether he is single or married—but women are defined by their relationship to men (by whether they are married or not). A way around this is to use "Ms." (which doesn't indicate marital status) to refer to women.

Sometimes we modify nouns that refer to jobs or positions to denote the sex of the person holding that position. This often done if the sex of the person holding the position goes against conventional expectations. To get a sense of these expectations, think about what sex you would instinctively assume the subject of each of these sentences to be:

The doctor walked into the room.

The nurse walked into the room.

Many people assume that doctors are men and that nurses

are women. Because of such assumptions, someone might write sentences like "The female doctor walked into the room" or "The male nurse walked into the room."

Using "female" and "male" in this way reinforces the assumption that most or all doctors are male and most or all nurses are female. Unless the sex of the nurse or doctor is important to the meaning of the sentence, it can be omitted.

As you work on becoming a gender-savvy writer, you may find it helpful to watch out for the following gendered nouns and replace them with one of the alternatives listed below. Check a thesaurus for alternatives to gendered nouns not included in this list.

gendered noun	**gender-neutral noun**
man	person, individual
freshman	first-year student
mankind	people, human beings, humanity
man-made	machine-made, synthetic
the common man	the average (or ordinary) person
to man	to operate, to cover, to staff
chairman	chair, chairperson, coordinator
mailman	mail carrier, letter carrier, postal worker
policeman	police officer
steward, stewardess	flight attendant
congressman	congress person, legislator, representative

Dear Sir:	Dear Sir or Madam:, Dear Editor:, Dear Service Representative:, To Whom it May Concern:

Proper Nouns

Proper nouns can also give gender-savvy writers pause, but as with common nouns, it is usually very easy to use gender-neutral language once you've noticed the gendered patterns in your own writing.

And the best way to avoid any confusion in your use of proper nouns is to use the same rules to discuss of women subjects as you already use when you're writing about men.

In the examples below, notice how using different conventions for references to male and female subjects suggests a difference in the amount of respect being given to individuals on the basis of their gender.

1. Refer to women subjects by only their last names—just as you would do for men subjects.

   For example, we would never refer to William Shakespeare as just "William;" we call him "Shakespeare" or "William Shakespeare." Thus, you should never refer to Jane Austen simply as "Jane;" you should write "Jane Austen" or "Austen."

2. In circumstances where you're writing about several people who have the same last name, try using the full name of the person every time you refer to him/her.

   For example, if you're writing about George and Martha Washington of United States, referring to him as

"Washington" and her as "Martha" conveys a greater respect for him than for her.

In order to express an equal amount of respect for these two historical figures, simply refer to each subject by her/his full name: "George Washington" and "Martha Washington." This option may sound like it could get too wordy, but it actually works very well in most situations.

3. Refer to women subjects by their full titles, just as you would refer to men subjects.

   For example, you wouldn't call American President Reagan "Ronald," so you wouldn't want to refer to British Prime Minister Thatcher as "Margaret." Simply call her "Prime Minister Thatcher," just as you would write "President Reagan" to refer to him.

Sex *versus* Gender

In many women's studies classes, one of the fundamental concepts students are expected to master is the difference feminists see between an individual's sex (which feminists understand as one's biological makeup—male, female, or intersexed) and that person's gender (a social construction based on sex—man/masculine or woman/feminine).

Because this distinction is so fundamental to understanding much of the material in many Women's Studies courses, expressing the difference between sex and gender is an important element in many writing assignments given by women's studies instructors.

Essentially, all you need to express sex vs. gender distinctions accurately in your writing is a clear understanding of the difference between sex and gender.

As you are writing, ask yourself whether what you're talking about is someone's biological makeup or something about the way that person has been socialized.

If you're referring to biology, use "male" or "female," and if what you're talking about has to do with a behavior or social role someone has been taught because of her/his biology, use "woman" or "man."

Thinking about the different answers to these two questions might help clarify the distinction between sex and gender:

What does it mean to be male?

What does it mean to be a man?

"To be male," as an expression of biological sex, is to have a chromosomal makeup of XY. "To be a man," however, expresses the socially constructed aspects of masculinity. Ideas of masculinity change across time, culture, and place.

Think about the differences between what it meant "to be a man" in 17th-century France versus what it means "to be a man" today in the United States.

Checklist for Gender Revisions

To ensure that you've used gender savvy language in your piece of writing, try asking yourself the following questions:

1. Have you used "man" or "men" or words containing one of them to refer to people who may be female? If so, consider substituting another word. For example, instead of "fireman," try "firefighter."
2. If you have mentioned someone's gender, was it necessary to do so? If you identify someone as a female architect, for example, do you (or would you) refer to someone else as a "male architect"?

And if you then note that the woman is an attractive blonde mother of two, do you mention that the man is a muscular, square-jawed father of three? Unless gender and related matters—looks, clothes, parenthood—are relevant to your point, leave them unmentioned.

3. Do you use any occupational stereotypes? Watch for the use of female pronouns for elementary school teachers and male ones for scientists, for example.
4. Do you use language that in any way shows a lack of respect for either sex?
5. Have you used "he," "him," "his," or "himself" to refer to people who may be female?

Understanding Assignments

The first step in any successful college writing venture is reading the assignment. While this sounds like a simple task, it can be a tough one. This analysis will help you unravel your assignment directions and help you begin to craft an effective response.

Much of the following advice will involve translating typical assignment terms and practices into meaningful clues to the type of writing your instructor expects.

Basic Beginnings

Consider adopting two habits that will serve you well—regardless of the assignment, department, or instructor:

1. Read the assignment carefully *as soon as you receive it*. Do not put this task off—reading the assignment at the beginning will save you time, stress, and problems later.

An assignment can look pretty straightforward at first, particularly if the instructor has provided lots of information. That does not mean it will not take time and effort to complete; you may even have to learn a new skill to complete the assignment.

2. Ask the instructor about *anything* you do not understand. Do not hesitate to approach your instructor. Instructors would prefer to set you straight *before* you hand the paper in. That's also when you will find their feedback most useful.

Assignment Formats

Many assignments follow a basic format. Assignments often begin with an overview of the topic, include a central verb or verbs that describe the task, and offer some additional suggestions, questions, or prompts to get you started:

1. An Overview of Some Kind

The instructor might set the stage with some general discussion of the subject of the assignment, introduce the topic, or remind you of something pertinent that you have discussed in class. For example:

"Throughout history, gerbils have played a key role in politics" or "In the last few weeks of class, we have focused on the evening wear of the housefly ..."

2. The Task of the Assignment

Pay attention; this part tells you what to do when you write the paper. Look for the key verb or verbs in the sentence. Words like *analyze*, *summarize*, or *compare* direct you to think about your topic in a certain way. Also pay attention to words such as *how*, *what*, *when*, *where*, and *why*; these words specify tasks.

"Analyze the effect that gerbils had on the Russian Revolution," or "Suggest an interpretation of housefly undergarments that differs from Darwin's."

3. Additional Material to Think About

Here you will find some questions to use as springboards as you begin to think about the topic. Instructors usually include these questions as *suggestions* rather than *requirements*. Do not feel compelled to answer every question unless the instructor asks you to do so. Pay attention to the order of the questions. Sometimes they suggest the thinking process your instructor imagines you will need to follow to begin thinking about the topic.

"You may wish to consider the differing views held by Communist gerbils *vs.* Monarchist gerbils," or "Can there be such a thing as 'the housefly garment industry' or is it just a home-based craft?"

4. Style Tips

These are the instructor's comments about writing expectations:

"Be concise," "Write effectively," or "Argue furiously."

5. Technical Details

These instructions usually indicate format rules or guidelines.

"Your paper must be typed in Palatino font on gray paper and must not exceed 600 pages. It is due on the anniversary of Mao Tsetung's death."

The assignment's parts may not appear in exactly this order, and each part may be very long *or* really short. Nonetheless, being aware of this standard pattern can help you understand what your instructor wants you to do.

Interpreting the Assignment

Ask yourself a few basic questions as you read and jot down the answers on the assignment sheet.

1. Why did your instructor ask you to do this particular task?
2. Who is your audience?
3. What kind of evidence do you need to support your ideas?
4. What kind of writing style is acceptable?
5. What are the absolute rules of the paper?

Try to look at the question from the point of view of the instructor. Recognize that your instructor has a reason for giving you this assignment and for giving it to you at a particular point in the semester.

In every assignment, the instructor has a challenge for you. This challenge could be anything from demonstrating an ability to think clearly to demonstrating an ability to use the library. See the assignment not as a vague suggestion of what to do but as an opportunity to show that you can handle the course material as directed.

Paper assignments give you more than a topic to discuss—they ask you to do something with the topic. Keep reminding yourself of that. Be careful to avoid the other extreme as well: do not read more into the assignment than what is there.

1. Why did your Instructor ask you to do this Particular Task?

Of course, your instructor has given you an assignment so that he or she will be able to assess your understanding of the course material and give you an appropriate grade. But there is more to it than that. Your instructor has tried to design a learning experience of some kind.

Your instructor wants you to think about something in a particular way for a particular reason. If you read the course description at the beginning of your syllabus, review the assigned readings, and consider the assignment itself, you may begin to see the plan, purpose, or approach to the subject matter that your instructor has created for you. If you still aren't sure of the assignment's goals, try asking the instructor.

Given your instructor's efforts, it helps to answer the question: What is my purpose in completing this assignment? Is it to gather research from a variety of outside sources and present a coherent picture?

Is it to take material I have been learning in class and apply it to a new situation? Is it to prove a point one way or another? Key words from the assignment can help you figure this out. Look for key terms in the form of *active verbs* that tell you what to do.

Key Terms: Finding those active verbs

Here are some common key words and definitions to help you think about assignment terms:

Information words ask you to demonstrate what you know about the subject, such as who, what, when, where, how, and why.

- **Define**—Give the subject's meaning (according to someone or something). Sometimes you have to give more than one view on the subject's meaning.
- **Explain**—Give reasons why or examples of how something happened.
- **Illustrate**—Give descriptive examples of the subject and show how each is connected with the subject.

- **Summarize**—Briefly list the important ideas you learned about the subject.
- **Trace**—Outline how something has changed or developed from an earlier time to its current form.
- **Research**—Gather material from outside sources about the subject, often with the implication or requirement that you will analyze what you have found.

Relation words ask you to demonstrate how things are connected.

- **Compare**—Show how two or more things are similar (and, sometimes, different).
- **Contrast**—Show how two or more things are dissimilar.
- **Apply**—Use details that you've been given to demonstrate how an idea, theory, or concept works in a particular situation.
- **Cause**—Show how one event or series of events made something else happen.
- **Relate**—Show or describe the connections between things.

Interpretation words ask you to defend ideas of your own about the subject. Do not see these words as requesting opinion alone (unless the assignment specifically says so), but as requiring opinion that is supported by concrete evidence.

Remember examples, principles, definitions, or concepts from class or research and use them in your interpretation.

- **Assess**—Summarize your opinion of the subject and measure it against something.
- **Prove, justify**—Give reasons or examples to demonstrate how or why something is the truth.

- **Evaluate, respond**—State your opinion of the subject as good, bad, or some combination of the two, with examples and reasons.
- **Support**—Give reasons or evidence for something you believe (be sure to state clearly what it is that you believe).
- **Synthesize** —Put two or more things together that have not been put together in class or in your readings before; do not just summarize one and then the other and say that they are similar or different—you must provide a reason for putting them together that runs all the way through the paper.
- **Analyze**—Determine how individual parts create or relate to the whole, figure out how something works, what it might mean, or why it is important.
- **Argue**—Take a side and defend it with evidence against the other side.

More clues to your purpose

As you read the assignment, think about what the teacher does in class.

- What kinds of textbooks or coursepack did your teacher choose for the course—ones that provide background information, explain theories or perspectives, or argue a point of view?
- In lecture, does your teacher ask your opinion, try to prove her point of view, or use keywords that show up again in the assignment?
- What kinds of assignments are typical in this discipline? Social science classes often expect more research. Humanities classes thrive on interpretation and analysis.
- How do the assignments, readings, and lectures work

together in the course? Teachers spend time designing courses, sometimes even arguing with their peers about the most effective course materials.

Figuring out the overall design to the course will help you understand what each assignment is meant to achieve.

2. Who is your Audience?

Now, what about your reader? Most undergraduates think of their audience as the instructor. True, your instructor is a good person to keep in mind as you write.

But for the purposes of a good paper, think of your audience as someone like your roommate: smart enough to understand a clear, logical argument, but not someone who already knows exactly what is going on in your particular paper.

Remember, even if the instructor knows everything there is to know about your paper topic, he or she still has to read *your* paper and assess *your* understanding.

In other words, *teach* the material to your reader. Aiming a paper at your audience happens in two ways: you make decisions about the tone and the level of information you want to convey.

- **Tone** means the "voice" of your paper. Should you be chatty, formal, or objective? Usually you will find some happy medium—you do not want to alienate your reader by sounding condescending or superior, but you do not want to, um, like, totally wig on the man, you know?

  Eschew ostentatious erudition: some students think the way to sound academic is to use big words. Be careful—you can sound ridiculous, especially if you use the *wrong* big words.

- The **level of information** you use depends on who you think your audience is.

  If you imagine your audience as your teacher and he already knows everything you have to say, you may find yourself leaving out key information that can cause your argument to be unconvincing and illogical.

  But you do not have to explain every single word or issue. If you are telling your roommate what happened on the *X-Files* last night, you do not say, "First Mulder walked into the room.

  Then the purple, well-shod alien turned around. Then Mulder smiled slightly. A clock was ticking." You also do not say, "This guy found some aliens. The end." Find some balance of useful details that support your main point.

The Grim Truth

With a few exceptions (including some lab and ethnography reports), you are probably being asked to make an argument. You must convince your audience.

It is easy to forget this aim when you are researching and writing; as you become involved in your subject matter, you may become enmeshed in the details and focus on learning or simply telling the information you have found. You need to do more than just repeat what you have read.

Your writing should have a point, and you should be able to say it in a sentence. Sometimes teachers call this sentence a "thesis" or a "claim."

So, if your teacher tells you to write about some aspect of oral hygiene, you do not want to just list: "First, you brush your teeth with a soft brush and some peanut butter. Then, you floss with unwaxed, bologna-flavoured string.

Finally, gargle with bourbon." Instead, you could say, "Of all the oral cleaning methods, sandblasting removes the most plaque.

Therefore, it should be recommended by the "Dental Association." Or, "From an aesthetic perspective, moldy teeth can be quite charming. However, their joys are short-lived."

Convincing the reader of your argument is the goal of academic writing. It doesn't have to say "argument" anywhere in the assignment for you to need one.

Look at the assignment and think about what kind of argument you could make about it instead of just seeing it as a checklist of information you have to present.

3. What Kind of Evidence do you Need?

There are lots of different types of proof or evidence. Here are several common types:

- **Einstein proof**—A famous (or not so famous) smart person agrees with you or says something you can use to back up your point. This kind of evidence can come from course materials or outside research. Be sure to cite these scholars as sources.
- **Case proof**—A case in which your point works or the other person's point does not work to demonstrate your idea.

  These may come from your experience, hypothetical situations, or from outside sources.
- **Fact proof**—Statistics, "objective" information. You will need lots of documentation here and probably several trips to the library.
- **For example proof**—Examples from the subject or text you are studying to back up your *focused* point. For example

(!), you might use Ophelia's scenes to explain Hamlet's depression.

Professors will usually tell you what kind of proof they want. If the assignment tells you to "do research," head quickly to the library.

Make sure you are clear about this part of the assignment, because your use of evidence will be crucial in writing a successful paper. You are not just learning how to argue; you are learning how to argue with specific types of materials and ideas.

4. What Kind of Writing Style is Acceptable?

You cannot always tell from the assignment just what sort of writing style your teacher expects. The teacher may be really laid back in class but still expect you to sound formal in writing.

Or the teacher may be fairly formal in class and ask you to write a reflection paper where you need to use "I" and speak from your own experience.

Try to avoid false associations of a particular field with a style ("art historians like wacky creativity," or "political scientists are boring and just give facts") and look instead to the types of readings you have been given in class.

No one expects you to write like Plato—just use the readings as a guide for what is standard or preferable to your instructor. When in doubt, ask your instructor about the level of formality she expects.

No matter what field you are writing for or what facts you are including, if you do not write so that your reader can understand your main idea, you have wasted your time. So make *clarity* your main goal.

5. Technical Details about the Assignment

The technical information you are given in an assignment always seems like the easy part. This section can actually give you lots of little hints about approaching the task. Find out if elements such as page length and citation format are negotiable.

Some professors do not have strong preferences as long as you are consistent and fully answer the assignment. Some professors are very specific and will deduct big points for deviations.

Usually, the page length tells you something important: The teacher thinks the size of the paper is appropriate to the assignment's parameters. In plain English, your teacher is telling you how many pages it *should* take for you to answer the question as fully as you are expected to.

So if an assignment is two pages long, you cannot pad your paper with examples or reword your main idea several times. Hit your one point early, defend it with the clearest example, and finish quickly.

If an assignment is ten pages long, you can be more complex in your main points and examples—and if you can only produce five pages for that assignment, you need to see someone for help—pronto.

Tricks that don't work

Your teachers are not fooled when you:

- **Spend more time on the cover page than the essay**—Graphics, cool binders, and cute titles are no replacement for a well-written paper.
- **Use huge fonts, wide margins, or extra spacing to pad the page length**—These tricks are immediately

obvious to the eye. Most instructors use the same word processor you do. They know what's possible.

Such tactics are especially damning when the teacher has a stack of 60 papers to grade and yours is the only one that low-flying airplane pilots could read.

- **Use a paper from another class that covered "sort of similar" material.** Again, the instructor has a particular task for you to fulfil in the assignment that usually relates to course material and lectures. Your other paper may not cover this material. Ask the teacher—it can't hurt.
- **Get all wacky and "creative" before you answer the question.** Showing that you are able to think beyond the boundaries of a simple assignment can be good, but you must do what the assignment calls for first.

  Again, check with your teacher. A humorous tone can be refreshing for someone grading a stack of papers, but it will not get you a good grade if you have not fulfilled the task.

Critical reading of assignments leads to skills in other types of reading and writing. If you get good at figuring out what the real goals of assignments are, you are going to be better at understanding the goals of all of your classes and fields of study.

■■■

CHAPTER 4

Structure of a Sentence

In the field of linguistics, a **sentence** is an expression in natural language, and often defined to indicate a grammatical unit consisting of one or more words that generally bear minimal syntactic relation to the words that precede or follow it. A sentence can include words grouped meaningfully to express a statement, question, exclamation, request or command.

As with all language expressions, sentences may contain both function and content words, and contain properties distinct to natural language, such as characteristic intonation and timing patterns.

Sentences are generally characterized in most languages by the presence of a finite verb, e.g. "The quick brown fox *jumps* over the lazy dog".

Components of a Sentence

Clauses

A clause consists of a *subject* and a *predicate*. The subject is typically a noun phrase, though other kinds of phrases (such as gerund phrases) work as well, and some languages allow subjects to be omitted. The predicate is a finite verb phrase: a finite verb together with zero or more objects, zero or more complements, and zero or more adverbials.

There are two types of clauses: *independent* and *subordinate (dependent)*. An independent clause demonstrates a complete thought; it is a complete sentence: for example, "I am sad." A subordinate clause is not a complete sentence: for example, "because I had to move."

Complete Sentences

A simple complete sentence consists of a single clause (subject and predicate). Other complete sentences consist of two or more clauses.

Classification

By Structure

One traditional scheme for classifying English sentences is by the number and types of finite clauses:

- A *simple sentence* consists of a single independent clause with no dependent clauses.
- A *compound sentence* consists of multiple independent clauses with no dependent clauses. These clauses are joined together using conjunctions, punctuation, or both.
- A *complex sentence* consists of at least one independent clause and one dependent clause.
- A *complex-compound sentence* (or *compound-complex sentence*) consists of multiple independent clauses, at least one of which has at least one dependent clause.

By Purpose

Sentences can also be classified based on their purpose:

- A *declarative sentence* or declaration, the most common type, commonly makes a statement: "I am going home."
- An *interrogative sentence* or question is commonly used to request information — "When are you going to work?" — but sometimes not.
- An *exclamative sentence* or exclamation is generally a more emphatic form of statement expressing emotion: "What a wonderful day this is!"
- An *imperative sentence* or command tells someone to do something: "Go to work at 7:30 in the morning."

Major and Minor Sentences

A major sentence is a *regular* sentence; it has a subject and a predicate. For example: *I have a ball.* In this sentence one can change the persons: *We have a ball.* However, a minor sentence is an irregular type of sentence. It does not contain a finite verb. For example, "Mary!" "Yes." "Coffee." etc. Other examples of minor sentences are headings (e.g. the heading of this entry), stereotyped expressions (*Hello!*), emotional expressions (*Wow!*), proverbs, etc. This can also include nominal sentences like *The more, the merrier*. These do not contain verbs in order to intensify the meaning around the nouns and are normally found in poetry and catchphrases.

Sentences that comprise a single word are called word sentences, and the words themselves sentence words.

Remember that every clause is, in a sense, a miniature sentence. A simple sentences contains only a single clause, while a compound sentence, a complex sentence, or a compound-complex sentence contains at least two clauses.

The Simple Sentence

The most basic type of sentence is the **simple sentence**, which contains only one clause. A simple sentence can be as short as one word:

Run!

Usually, however, the sentence has a subject as well as a predicate and both the subject and the predicate may have modifiers. All of the following are simple sentences, because each contains only one clause:

Melt!

Ice **melts**.

The ice **melts** quickly.

The ice on the river **melts** quickly under the warm May sun.

Lying exposed without its blanket of snow, the ice on the river **melts** quickly under the warm May sun.

As you can see, a simple sentence can be quite long — it is a mistake to think that you can tell a simple sentence from a compound sentence or a complex sentence simply by its length.

The most natural sentence structure is the simple sentence: it is the first kind which children learn to speak, and it remains by far the most common sentence in the spoken language of people of all ages. In written work, simple sentences can be very effective for grabbing a reader's attention or for summing up an argument, but you have to use them with care: too many simple sentences can make your writing seem childish.

When you do use simple sentences, you should add transitional phrases to connect them to the surrounding sentences.

The Compound Sentence

A **compound sentence** consists of two or more independent clauses (or simple sentences) joined by co-ordinating conjunctions like "and," "but," and "or":

Simple

Canada is a rich country.

Simple

Still, it has many poor people.

Compound

Canada is a rich country, **but** still it has many poor people.

Compound sentences are very natural for English speakers — small children learn to use them early on to connect their ideas and to avoid pausing (and allowing an adult to interrupt):

Today at school Mr. Mohan brought in his pet rabbit, and he showed it to the class, and I got to pet it, and Karan held it, and we coloured pictures of it, and it ate part of my carrot at lunch, and ...

Of course, this is an extreme example, but if you over-use compound sentences in written work, your writing might seem immature.

A compound sentence is most effective when you use it to create a sense of balance or contrast between two (or more) equally-important pieces of information:

Bengaluru has better clubs, but **Mumbai has better cinemas**.

Special Cases of Compound Sentences

There are two special types of compound sentences which you

might want to note. First, rather than joining two simple sentences together, a co-ordinating conjunction sometimes joins two complex sentences, or one simple sentence and one complex sentence. In this case, the sentence is called a **compound-complex sentence**:

Compound-complex

The package arrived in the morning, but **the courier left before I could check the contents.**

The second special case involves punctuation. It is possible to join two originally separate sentences into a compound sentence using a semicolon instead of a co-ordinating conjunction:

Mr. Suresh Sharma had a serious drinking problem; when sober, however, he could be a formidable foe in the business.

Usually, a conjunctive adverb like "however" or "consequently" will appear near the beginning of the second part; but it is not required:

The sun rises in the east; it sets in the west.

The Complex Sentence

A **complex sentence** contains one independent clause and at least one dependent clause. Unlike a compound sentence, however, a complex sentence contains clauses which are ***not*** equal. Consider the following examples:

Simple

My friend invited me to a party. I do not want to go.

Compound

My friend invited me to a party, but I do not want to go.

Complex

Although my friend invited me to a party, I do not want to go.

In the first example, there are two separate simple sentences: "My friend invited me to a party" and "I do not want to go." The second example joins them together into a single sentence with the co-ordinating conjunction "but," but both parts could still stand as independent sentences — they are entirely equal, and the reader cannot tell which is most important. In the third example, however, the sentence has changed quite a bit: the first clause, "Although my friend invited me to a party," has become incomplete, or a dependent clause.

A complex sentence is very different from a simple sentence or a compound sentence because it makes clear which ideas are most important. When you write

My friend invited me to a party. I do not want to go.

or even

My friend invited me to a party, but I do not want to go.

The reader will have trouble knowing which piece of information is most important to you. When you write the subordinating conjunction "although" at the beginning of the first clause, however, you make it clear that the fact that your friend invited you is less important than, or **subordinate**, to the fact that you do not want to go.

■■■

CHAPTER 5

Punctuation

Punctuation is the name for marks used in writing. These marks help with understanding. There are many kinds of punctuation. Some of them can do many things. These are some common punctuation marks used in English:

- . is a period or full stop.
- , is a comma.
- ? is a question mark or query.
- ! is an exclamation mark.
- ‘ is an apostrophe.
- “ is a quotation mark.
- : is a colon.
- ; is a semicolon.
- ... is an ellipsis.
- - is a hyphen

The following sections will help you understand and use different types of punctuation more effectively in your writing.

We'll begins with the comma, the **punctuation** mark which usually causes writers the most trouble, before turning to other types of punctuation.

The Comma

Comma usage is in some respects a question of personal writing style: some writers use commas liberally, while others prefer to use them sparingly.

Most modern style guides now recommend using fewer commas rather than more, so when faced with the option of using a comma or not, you may find it wise to refrain.

For instance, the use of a comma before the "and" in a series is usually optional, and many writers choose to eliminate it, provided there is no danger of misreading:

We bought scarves, mittens and sweaters before leaving for Hillstation. (comma unnecessary before "and")

We ate apples, plums, and strawberry and kiwi compote. (comma needed before "and" for clarity)

Comma Usage

1. Use a comma before a co-ordinating conjunction that joins independent clauses (unless the independent clauses are very short):

   I wrapped the fresh fish in three layers of newspaper, but my van still smelled like trout for the next week. (commas with two independent clauses)

   She invited him to her party and he accepted. (comma unnecessary with short clauses)

2. Use a comma after an introductory adverb clause and,

often, after an introductory phrase (unless the phrase is very short):

After the hospital had completed its fund-raising campaign, an anonymous donor contributed an additional Rs.10,000. (after introductory adverb clause)

From the east wall to the west, her cottage measures twenty feet. (after introductory prepositional phrase)

In the bottom drawer you will find some pink spandex tights. (no comma with short, closely related phrase)

3. Use a comma to separate items in a series:

   Playing in a band can be exciting, but many people do not realize the hardships involved: constant rehearsals, playing until 2 a.m., handling drunken audience members, and transporting heavy equipment to and from gigs. (the comma preceding "and" is optional unless needed to prevent misreading)

4. Use commas to set off **non-restrictive elements** and other parenthetical elements. A **non-restrictive modifier** is a phrase or clause that does not restrict or limit the meaning of the word it is modifying. It is, in a sense, interrupting material that adds extra information to a sentence. Even though removing the non-restrictive element would result in some loss of meaning, the sentence would still make sense without it. You should usually set off non-restrictive elements with commas:

   The people of Haiti, who for decades have lived with grinding poverty and mind-numbing violence, are unfamiliar with the workings of a true democracy.

   A **restrictive modifier** is a phrase or clause that limits the meaning of what it modifies and is essential to the basic idea expressed in the sentence. You should not set off **restrictive elements** with commas:

Those residents of Ottawa who do not hold secure, well-paying jobs must resent the common portrayal of the city as a land of opportunity.

Note that you can use two other punctuation marks to set off non-restrictive elements or other **parenthetical information: parentheses** and dashes. Enclosing parenthetical information in parentheses reduces the importance of that information:

Mr. Grundy's driving record (with one small exception) was exemplary.

5. Placing parenthetical information between dashes has the opposite effect: it emphasises the material:

Mr. Grundy's driving record — with one exception — was exemplary.

Nevertheless, you should usually set off parenthetical information with commas.

Superfluous Commas

Equally important in understanding how to use commas effectively is knowing when *not* to use them. While this decision is sometimes a matter of personal taste, there are certain instances when you should definitely avoid a comma.

- Do not use a comma to separate the subject from its predicate:

  [Wrong] Registering for our fitness programmes before September 15, will save you thirty per cent of the membership cost.

[Right] Registering for our fitness programmes before September 15 will save you thirty per cent of the membership cost.

- Do not use a comma to separate a verb from its object or its subject complement, or a preposition from its object:

[Wrong] I hope to mail to you before Christmas, a current snapshot of my dog Benji.

She travelled around the world with, a small backpack, a bedroll, a pup tent and a camera.

[Right] I hope to mail to you before Christmas a current snapshot of my dog Benji.

[Right] She travelled around the world with a small backpack, a bedroll, a pup tent and a camera.

- Do not misuse a comma after a co-ordinating conjunction:

[Wrong] Sleet fell heavily on the tin roof but, the family was used to the noise and paid it no attention.

[Right] Sleet fell heavily on the tin roof, but the family was used to the noise and paid it no attention.

- Do not use commas to set off words and short phrases (especially introductory ones) that are not parenthetical or that are very slightly so:

[Wrong] After dinner, we will play badminton.

[Right] After dinner we will play badminton.

- Do not use commas to set off restrictive elements:

[Wrong] The fingers, on his left hand, are bigger than those on his right.

[Right] The fingers on his left hand are bigger than those on his right.

- Do not use a comma before the first item or after the last item of a series:

  [Wrong] The treasure chest contained, three wigs, some costume jewellery and Rs. 2 Lakh in Monopoly money.

  [Wrong] You should practice your punches, kicks and foot sweeps, if you want to improve in the martial arts.

  [Right] The treasure chest contained three wigs, some costume jewellery and Rs. 2 Lakh in Monopoly money.

  [Right] You should practice your punches, kicks and foot sweeps if you want to improve in the martial arts.

The Semicolon

You will usually use the **semicolon** to link independent clauses not joined by a co-ordinating conjunction. Semicolons should join only those independent clauses that are closely related in meaning.

Abdominal exercises help prevent back pain; proper posture is also important.

The auditors made six recommendations; however, only one has been adopted so far.

Do not use a semicolon to link a dependent clause or a phrase to an independent clause.

[Wrong] Although gaining and maintaining a high level of physical fitness takes a good deal of time; the effort pays off in the long run.

[Right] Although gaining and maintaining a high level of physical fitness takes a good deal of time, the effort pays off in the long run.

Generally, you should not place a semicolon before a coordinating conjunction that links two independent clauses. The only exception to this guideline is if the two independent clauses are very long and already contain a number of commas.

[Wrong] The economy has been sluggish for four years now; but some signs of improvement are finally beginning to show.

[Right] The economy has been sluggish for four years now, but some signs of improvement are finally beginning to show.

It may be useful to remember that, for the most part, you should use a semicolon only where you could also use a period.

There is one exception to this guideline. When punctuating a list or series of elements in which one or more of the elements contains an internal comma, you should use semicolons instead of commas to separate the elements from one another:

Harish mother believes three things: that every situation, no matter how grim, will be happily resolved; that no one knows more about human nature than she; and that Harish, who is thirty-five years old, will never be able to do his own laundry.

Quotation Marks

The exact rules for **quotation marks** vary greatly from language to language and even from country to country within the English-speaking world. In North American usage, you should place double quotation marks (") before and after directly quoted material and words of dialogue:

One critic ended his glowing review with this superlative: "It is simply the best film ever made about potato farming."

May replied, "This is the last cookie."

You also use quotation marks to set off certain titles, usually those of minor or short works — essays, short stories, short poems, songs, articles in periodicals, etc. For titles of longer works and separate publications, you should use italics (or underlined, if italics are not available). Use italics for titles of books, magazines, periodicals, newspapers, films, plays, long poems, long musical works, and television and radio programmes.

Once when I was sick, my father read me a story called "The Happy Flower," which was later made into a movie entitled *Flower Child*, starring Tiny Tim.

Sometimes, you will use quotation marks to set off words specifically referred to as terms, though some publishers prefer italics:

I know you like the word "unique," but do you really have to use it ten times in one essay?

"Well" is sometimes a noun, sometimes an adverb, sometimes an adjective and sometimes a verb.

Quotations Marks with other Punctuation

One question that frequently arises with quotation marks is where to place other punctuation marks in relation to them. Again, these rules vary from region to region:

1. Commas and periods always go inside the quotation marks.

   I know you are fond of the story "Children of the Corn," but is it an appropriate subject for your essay?

   "At last," said the old woman, "I can say I am truly happy."

2. Semicolons and colons always go outside the quotation marks.

   She never liked the poem "Dover Beach"; in fact, it was her least favourite piece of Victorian literature.

   He clearly states his opinion in the article "Of Human Bondage": he believes that television has enslaved and diminished an entire generation.

3. Question marks, exclamation marks, and dashes go inside quotation marks when they are part of the quotation, and outside when they do not.

   Where is your copy of "The Raven"?

   "How cold is it outside?" my mother asked.

   Note that in usage, you should use single quotation marks (') only to set off quoted material (or a minor title) inside a quotation.

   "I think she said `I will try,' not `I won't try,'" explained Saurav.

The Apostrophe

You should use an **apostrophe** to form the possessive case of a noun or to show that you have left out letters in a **contraction**. Note that you should not generally use contractions in formal, academic writing.

The convertible's engine has finally died. (The noun "convertible's" is in the possessive case)

I haven't seen my roommate for two weeks. (The verb "haven't" is a contraction of "have not")

To form the possessive of a plural noun ending in "s," simply place an apostrophe after the "s."

He has his three sons' futures in mind.

In many suburbs, the houses' designs are too much alike.

Possessive pronouns — for example, "hers," "yours," and "theirs" — do not take apostrophes. This is the case for the possessive pronoun "its" as well: when you write "it's" with an apostrophe, you are writing a contraction for "it is."

The spaceship landed hard, damaging its radar receiver. ("its" is the possessive pronoun)

It's your mother on the phone. ("it's" is the contraction of "it is")

Rules to using Apostrophes

Rule 1. Use the apostrophe with contractions. The apostrophe is always placed at the spot where the letter(s) has been removed.

Examples: don't, isn't

You're right.

She's a great teacher.

Rule 2. Use the apostrophe to show possession. Place the apostrophe before the s to show singular possession.

Examples: one boy's hat

one woman's hat

one actress's hat

one child's hat

Note: Although names ending in s or an s sound are not required to have the second s added in possessive form, it is preferred.

Mr. Jay golf clubs

Delhi's weather

Ms. Sunita's daughter

Khajurao's art work

Dr. Raman's appointment (name is Raman)

Mrs. Usha's books (name is Usha)

Rule 3. Use the apostrophe where the noun that should follow is implied.

Example: This was his father's, not his, jacket.

Rule 4. To show plural possession, make the noun plural first. Then immediately use the apostrophe.

Examples: two boys' hats

two women's hats

two actresses' hats

two children's hats

the Chuggs' house

the Jays' golf clubs

the Sunitas' daughter

the Khajuraos' art work

the Ramans' appointment

the Ushas' books

Rule 5. Do not use an apostrophe for the plural of a name.

Examples: We visited the Khajuraos in Gawalior.

The Chugg have two cats and a dog.

Rule 6. With a singular compound noun, show possession with 's at the end of the word.

Example: my mother-in-law's hat

Rule 7. If the compound noun is plural, form the plural first and then use the apostrophe.

Example: my two brothers-in-law's hats

Rule 8. Use the apostrophe and s after the second name only if two people possess the same item.

Examples: Varun and Manisha's home is constructed of redwood.

Varun's and Manisha's job contracts will be renewed next year.

Indicates separate ownership.

Varun and Manisha's job contracts will be renewed next year.

Indicates joint ownership of more than one contract.

Rule 9. Never use an apostrophe with possessive pronouns: his, hers, its, theirs, ours, yours, whose. They already show possession so they do not require an apostrophe.

Examples: This book is hers, not yours.

Incorrect: Sincerely your's.

Rule 10. The only time an apostrophe is used for it's is when it is a contraction for it is or it has.

Examples: It's a nice day.

It's your right to refuse the invitation.

It's been great getting to know you.

Rule 11. The plurals for capital letters and numbers used as nouns are not formed with apostrophes.

Examples: She consulted with three M.Ds

BUT

She went to three M.Ds' offices.

The apostrophe is needed here to show plural possessive.

She learned her ABCs.

the 1990s not the 1990's

the '90s or the mid-'70s not the '90's or the mid-'70's

She learned her times tables for 6s and 7s.

Exception: Use apostrophes with capital letters and numbers when the meaning would be unclear otherwise.

Examples: Please dot your i's.

You don't mean is.

Ted couldn't distinguish between her 6's and 0's.

You don't mean Os.

Rule 12. Use the possessive case in front of a gerund (-ing word).

Examples: Alex's skating was a joy to behold.

This does not stop Joan's inspecting of our facilities next Thursday.

Rule 13. If the gerund has a pronoun in front of it, use the possessive form of that pronoun.

Examples: I appreciate your inviting me to dinner.

I appreciated his working with me to resolve the conflict.

The Dash

As noted in the section on commas, you can use a **dash** at the beginning and end of parenthetical information. Usually, you will use dashes when you want to emphasise the information, but you might also use them if the parenthetical information is too long or abrupt to be set off with commas.

I think you would look fine wearing either the silk blouse — the one with the blue pattern — or the angora sweater. (abrupt interruption)

The idea of returning to the basics in the classroom — a notion which, incidentally, has been quietly supported for years by many respected teachers — is finally gaining some currency with school administrators. (lengthy interruption containing internal commas)

You can use a dash to conclude a list of elements, focusing them all toward one point.

Chocolate, cream, honey and peanut butter — all go into this fabulously rich dessert.

Dashes also mark sharp turns in thought.

We pored over exotic, mouth-watering menus from Nemo Catering, Menu du Jour, Taste Temptations, and three other reputable caterers — and rejected them all.

■■■

CHAPTER 6

Understanding the Audience and Getting Feedback

Audience

Audience Matters

When you're in the process of writing a paper, it's easy to forget that you are actually writing to someone.

Whether you've thought about it consciously or not, you always write to an audience: sometimes your audience is a very generalized group of readers, sometimes you know the individuals who compose the audience, and sometimes you write for yourself.

Keeping your audience in mind while you write can help you make good decisions about what material to include, in what order to organize your ideas, and how best to support your argument.

To illustrate the impact of audience, imagine you're writing a letter to your grandma to tell her about your first month of college. What details and stories might you include? What might you leave out?

Now imagine that you're writing on the same topic but your audience is your best friend. Unless you have an extremely cool grandma to whom you're very close, it's likely that your two letters would look quite different in terms of content, structure, and even tone.

Isn't my Instructor my Audience?

Yes, your instructor is probably the actual audience for your paper. Your instructors read and grade your essays, and you want to keep their needs and perspectives in mind when you write.

However, when you write an essay with only your instructor in mind, you might not say as much as you should or say it as clearly as you should, because you assume that the person grading it knows more than you do and will fill in the gaps.

This leaves it up to the instructor to decide what you are really saying, and she might decide differently than you expect. For example, she might decide that those gaps show that you don't know and understand the material.

Remember that time when you said to yourself, "I don't have to explain communism; my instructor knows more about that than I do" and got back a paper that said something like "Shows no understanding of communism"?

That's an example of what can go awry when you think of your instructor as your only audience.

Thinking about your audience differently can improve your writing, especially in terms of how clearly you express your argument. The clearer your points are, the more likely you are to have a strong essay.

Your instructor will say, "She really understands communism—she's able to explain it simply and clearly!" By treating your instructor as an intelligent but uninformed audience, you end up addressing her more effectively.

How do I Identify my Audience and What they Want from Me?

Before you even begin the process of writing, take some time to consider who your audience is and what they want from you. Use the following questions to help you identify your audience and what you can do to address its wants and needs.

- Who is your audience?
- How many audiences do you have? List them.
- What does your audience need? What do they want?
- What is most important to them?
- What are they least likely to care about?
- How might you organize your essay in a way that will be best for your audience?
- What do you have to say or what are you doing in your research that might surprise your audience?
- What do you want your audience to think, learn, or assume about you? What impression do you want your writing or your research to convey?

How much should I Explain?

This is the hard part. As we said earlier, you want to show your instructor that you know the material. But different assignments call for varying degrees of information. Different fields also have different expectations. The best place to start figuring out how much you should say about each part of your paper is in a careful reading of the assignment.

The assignment may specify an audience for your paper; sometimes the instructor will ask you to imagine that you are writing to your congressperson, for a professional journal, to a group of specialists in a particular field, or for a group of your peers.

If the assignment doesn't specify an audience, you may find it most useful to imagine your classmates reading the paper, rather than your instructor.

Now, knowing your imaginary audience, what other clues can you get from the assignment? If the assignment asks you to summarize something that you have read, then your reader wants you to include more examples from the text than if the assignment asks you to interpret the passage.

Most assignments in college focus on argument rather than the repetition of learned information, so your reader probably doesn't want a lengthy, detailed, point-by-point summary of your reading (book reports in some classes and argument reconstructions in philosophy classes are big exceptions to this rule).

If your assignment asks you to interpret or analyze the text (or an event or idea), then you want to make sure that your explanation of the material is focused and not so detailed that you end up spending more time on examples than on your analysis.

Once you have a draft, try your level of explanation out on a friend, a classmate, or a Writing Centre tutor. Get the person to read your rough draft, and then ask her to talk to you about what she did and didn't understand. (Now is not the time to talk about proofreading stuff, so make sure she ignores those issues for the time being). You will likely get one of the following responses or a combination of them:

- If your listener/reader has tons of questions about what you are saying, then you probably need to explain more. Let's say you are writing a paper on piranhas, and your reader says, "What's a piranha? Why do I need to know about them? How would I identify one?"

  Those are vital questions that you clearly need to answer in your paper. You need more detail and elaboration.

- On the other hand, if your reader gets confused, you probably need to explain more clearly. So if she says, "Are there piranhas in the lake around here?" you may not need to give more examples, but rather focus on making sure your examples and points are clear.

- If your reader looks bored and can repeat back to you more details than she needs to know to get your point, you probably explained too much.

  Excessive detail can also be confusing, because it can bog the reader down and keep her from focusing on your main points. You want your reader to say, "So it seems like your paper is saying that piranhas are misunderstood creatures that are essential to South American ecosystems," not "Piranhas are important."

- Sometimes it's not the amount of explanation that matters, but the word choice and tone you adopt. Your word choice and tone need to match your audience's expectations.

  For example, imagine you are researching piranhas; you find an article in *National Geographic* and another one in an academic journal for scientists. How would you expect the two articles to sound? *National Geographic* is written for a popular audience; you might expect it to have sentences like "The piranha generally lives in shallow rivers and streams in South America."

The scientific journal, on the other hand, might use much more technical language, because it's written for an audience of specialists.

A sentence like "*Serrasalmus piraya* lives in fresh and brackish intercoastal and proto-arboreal sub-tropical regions between the 45th and 38th parallels" might not be out of place in the journal.

Generally, you want your reader to know enough material to understand the points you are making. It's like the old forest/trees metaphor. If you give the reader nothing but trees, she won't see the forest.

If you give her a big forest and no trees, she won't know how you got to the forest (she might say, "Your point is fine, but you haven't proven it to me"). You want the reader to say, "Nice forest, and those trees really help me to see it."

Reading as a Writer

Writers tend to read over their own papers pretty quickly, with the knowledge of what they are trying to argue already in their minds. Reading in this way can cause you to skip over gaps in your written argument because the gap-filler is in your head.

A problem occurs when your reader falls into these gaps. Your reader wants you to make the necessary connections from one thought or sentence to the next.

When you don't, the reader can become confused or frustrated. Think about when you read something and you struggle to find the most important points or what the writer is trying to say. Isn't that annoying?

Doesn't it make you want to quit reading and surf the web or call a friend? A confused or frustrated reader is not your goal—you want the reader to say, "Yeah, I see what you are saying," not "What does that have to do with anything?"

A good writer does not hope for psychic readers; rather, she or he provides the information the reader needs to understand the paper. To locate trouble spots where you need to explain more, stop reading as a writer and start.

Reading as a Reader

Instead of reading your draft as if you wrote it and know what you meant, try reading it as if you have no previous knowledge of the material. Have you explained enough? Are the connections clear? This can be hard to do at first. Consider using one of the following strategies:

- Take a break from your work—go work out, take a nap, take a day off. This is why the Writing Centre encourages you to start writing more than a day before the paper is due.

  If you write the paper the night before it's due, you make it almost impossible to read the paper with a fresh eye.

- Get a reader—find someone unfamiliar with the material to read your paper. Have him ignore all the little stuff like spelling and indentations and mark only the places where he doesn't understand why you are talking about something, how the information you are giving him relates to the other information, or what happened. Then explain those parts to him and see if that helps. If he says it helped, write what you said into the paper.

Remember, if your roommate doesn't understand your paper, your instructor might not either. We are happy to play the reader role for you here at the Writing Centre, so feel free to choose us as your reader.

- Try outlining after writing—after you have a draft, look at each paragraph separately. Write down the main point for each paragraph on a separate sheet of paper, in the order you have put them.

  Then look at your "outline"—does it reflect what you meant to say, in a logical order? Are some paragraphs hard to reduce to one point? Why? This technique will help you find places where you may have confused your reader by straying from your original plan for the paper.

- Read the paper aloud—we do this all the time at the Writing Center, and once you get used to it, you'll see that it helps you slow down and really consider how your reader experiences your text.

  It will also help you catch a lot of sentence-level errors, such as misspellings and missing words, which can make it difficult for your reader to focus on your argument.

These techniques can help you read your paper in the same way your reader will and make revisions that help your reader understand your argument.

Then, when your instructor finally reads your finished draft, she or he won't have to fill in any gaps. The more work you do, the less work your audience will have to do—and the more likely it is that your instructor will follow and understand your argument.

Getting Feedback

Sometimes you'd like feedback from someone else about your

writing, but you may not be sure how to get it. This analysis describes when, where, how and from whom you might receive effective responses as you develop as a writer.

Why get Feedback on your Writing?

You'll become a better writer, and writing will become a less painful process. When might you need feedback? You might be just beginning a paper and want to talk to someone else about your ideas. You might be midway through a draft and find that you are unsure about the direction you've decided to take.

You might wonder why you received a lower grade than you expected on a paper, or you might not understand the comments that professor has written in the margins. Essentially, asking for feedback at any stage helps you break out of the isolation of writing. When you ask for feedback, you are no longer working in a void, wondering whether or not you understand the assignment and/or are making yourself understood. By seeking feedback from others, you are taking positive, constructive steps to improve your own writing and develop as a writer.

Why People don't ask for Feedback

- You worry that the feedback will be negative. Many people avoid asking others what they think about a piece of writing because they have a sneaking suspicion that the news will not be good. If you want to improve your writing, however, constructive criticism from others will help. Remember that the criticism you receive is only criticism of the *writing* and not of the *writer*.
- You don't know whom to ask. The person who can offer the most effective feedback on your writing may vary

depending on when you need the feedback and what kind of feedback you need.

Keep in mind, though, that if you are really concerned about a piece of writing, almost any thoughtful reader (e.g., your roommate, your mother, your brother, etc.) can provide useful feedback that will help you improve your writing. Don't wait for the expert; share your writing often and with a variety of readers.

- You don't know how to ask. It can be awkward to ask for feedback, even if you know whom you want to ask. Asking someone, "Could you take a look at my paper?" or "Could you tell me if this is OK?" can sometimes elicit wonderfully rich responses.

  Usually, though, you need to be specific about where you are in the writing process and the kind of feedback that would help. You might say, "I'm really struggling with the organization of this paper. Could you read these paragraphs and see if the ideas seem to be in the right order?"

- You don't want to take up your teacher's time. You may be hesitant to go to your professor to talk about your writing because you don't want to bother him or her. The office hours that these busy people set aside, though, are reserved for your benefit, because the teachers on this campus want to communicate with students about their ideas and their work.

  Faculty can be especially generous and helpful with their advice when you drop by their office with specific questions and know the kinds of help you need. If you can't meet during the instructor's office hours, try making a special appointment. If you find that you aren't able to schedule a time to talk with your instructor, remember that there are plenty of other people around you who can offer feedback.

- You've gotten feedback in the past that was unhelpful. If earlier experiences haven't proved satisfactory, try again. Ask a different person, or ask for feedback in a new way.

  Experiment with asking for feedback at different stages in the writing process: when you are just beginning an assignment, when you have a draft, or when you think you are finished.

  Figure out when you benefit from feedback the most, the kinds of people you get the best feedback from, the kinds of feedback you need, and the ways to ask for that feedback effectively.

Possible Writing Moments for Feedback

There is no "best time" to get feedback on a piece of writing. In fact, it is often helpful to ask for feedback at several different stages of a writing project. Listed below are some parts of the writing process and some kinds of feedback you might need in each. Keep in mind, though, that every writer is different—you might think about these issues at other stages of the writing process, and that's fine.

- The beginning/idea stage: Do I understand the assignment? Am I gathering the right kinds of information to answer this question? Are my strategies for approaching this assignment effective ones? How can I discover the best way to develop my early ideas into a feasible draft?
- Outline/thesis: I have an idea about what I want to argue, but I'm not sure if it is an appropriate or complete response to this assignment. Is the way I'm planning to organize

my ideas working? Does it look like I'm covering all the bases? Do I have a clear main point? Do I know what I want to say to the reader?

- Rough draft: Does my paper make sense, and is it interesting? Have I proven my thesis statement? Is the evidence I'm using convincing? Is it explained clearly? Have I given the reader enough information? Does the information seem to be in the right order? What can I say in my introduction and conclusion?
- Early polished draft: Are the transitions between my ideas smooth and effective? Do my sentences make sense individually? How's my writing style?
- Late or final polished draft: Are there any noticeable spelling or grammar errors? Are my margins, footnotes, and formatting okay? Does the paper seem effective? Is there anything I should change at the last minute?
- After the fact: How should I interpret the comments on my paper? Why did I receive the grade I did? What else might I have done to strengthen this paper? What can I learn as a writer about this writing experience? What should I do the next time I have to write a paper?

A Note on Asking for Feedback After a Paper has been Graded

Many people go to see their professor after they receive a paper back with comments and a grade attached. If you seek feedback after your paper is returned to you, it makes sense to wait 24 hours before scheduling a meeting to talk about it. If you are angry or upset about a grade, the day off gives you time to calm down and put things in perspective.

More important, taking a day off allows you to read

through the instructor's comments and think about why you received the grade that you did.

You might underline or circle comments that were confusing to you so that you can ask about them later. You will also have an opportunity to reread your own writing and evaluate it more critically yourself.

After all, you probably haven't seen this piece of work since you handed it in a week or more ago, and refreshing your memory about its merits and weaknesses might help you make more sense of the grade and the instructor's comments.

Also, be prepared to separate the discussion of your grade from the discussion of your development as a writer. It is difficult to have a productive meeting that achieves both of these goals.

You may have very good reasons for meeting with an instructor to argue for a better grade, and having that kind of discussion is completely legitimate.

Be very clear with your instructor about your goals. Are you meeting to contest the grade your paper received and explain why you think the paper deserved a higher one? Are you meeting because you don't understand why your paper received the grade it did and would like clarification?

Or are you meeting because you want to use this paper and the instructor's comments to learn more about how to write in this particular discipline and do better on future written work?

Being up front about these distinctions can help you and your instructor know what to expect from the conference and avoid any confusion between the issue of grading and the issue of feedback.

Kinds of Feedback to Ask For

Asking for a specific kind of feedback can be the best way to get advice that you can use. Think about what kinds of topics you want to discuss and what kinds of questions you want to ask:

- Understanding the assignment (Do I understand the task? How long should it be? What kinds of sources should I be using?

  Do I have to answer all of the questions on the assignment sheet or are they just prompts to get me thinking? Are some parts of the assignment more important than other parts?)
- Factual content (Is my understanding of the course material accurate? Where else could I look for more information?)
- Interpretation/analysis (Do I have a point? Does my argument make sense? Is it logical and consistent? Is it supported by sufficient evidence?)
- Organization (Are my ideas in a useful order? Does the reader need to know anything else up front? Is there another way to consider ordering this information?)
- "Flow" (Do I have good transitions? Does the introduction prepare the reader for what comes later? Do my topic sentences accurately reflect the content of my paragraphs? Can the reader follow me?)
- Style (Comments on earlier papers can help you identify writing style issues that you might want to look out for. Is my writing style appealing? Do I use the passive voice too often? Are there too many "to be" verbs?)
- Grammar (Just as with style, comments on earlier papers will help you identify grammatical "trouble spots." Am I

using commas correctly? Do I have problems with subject-verb agreement?)

- Small errors (Is everything spelled right? Are there any typos?)

Possible Sources of Feedback and What they're Good For

Yourself

Believe it or not, you can learn to be your own best reader, particularly if you practice reading your work critically. First, think about writing problems that you know you have had in the past. Look over old papers for clues.

Then, give yourself some critical distance from your writing by setting it aside for a few hours, overnight, or even for a couple of days. Come back to it with a fresh eye, and you will be better able to offer yourself feedback.

Finally, be conscious of what you are reading for. You may find that you have to read your draft several times—perhaps once for content, once for organization and transitions, and once for style and grammar.

If you need feedback on a specific issue, such as passive voice, you may need to read through the draft one time alone focusing on that issue.

Whatever you do, don't count yourself out as a source of feedback. Remember that ultimately you care the most and will be held responsible for what appears on the page. It's your paper.

A Classmate (a familiar and knowledgeable reader)

When you need feedback from another person, a classmate can be an excellent source. A classmate knows the course material and can help you make sure you understand the course content. A classmate is probably also familiar with the sources that are available for the class and the specific assignment.

Moreover, you and your classmates can get together and talk about the kinds of feedback you both received on earlier work for the class, building your knowledge base about what the instructor is looking for in writing assignments.

Your expert Reader or TA (Teaching Assistant)

Your TA is an expert reader—he or she is working on an advanced degree, either a Master's or a Ph.D., in the subject area of your paper. Your TA is also either the primary teacher of the course or a member of the teaching team, so he or she probably had a hand in selecting the source materials, writing the assignment, and setting up the grading scheme.

No one knows what the TA is looking for on the paper better than the TA , and most of the TAs on campus would be happy to talk with you about your paper.

Your Professor (a very expert reader)

Your professor is the most expert reader you can find. He or she has a Ph.D. in the subject area that you are studying, and probably also wrote the assignment, either alone or with help from TAs. Like your TA, your professor can be the best source for information about what the instructor is looking for on the paper and may be your best guide in developing into a strong academic writer.

Your Roommate/friend/family member (an interested but not familiar reader)

It can be very helpful to get feedback from someone who doesn't know anything about your paper topic. These readers, because they are unfamiliar with the subject matter, often ask questions that help you realize what you need to explain further or that push you to think about the topic in new ways.

They can also offer helpful general writing advice, letting you know if your paper is clear or your argument seems well organized, for example. Ask them to read your paper and then summarize for you what they think its main points are.

The Writing Centre (an interested but not familiar reader with special training)

While the Writing Centre staff may not have specialized knowledge about your paper topic, our tutors are trained to assist you with your writing needs. We cannot edit or proofread for you, but we can help you identify problems and address them at any stage of the writing process.

Tutors in the Writing Centre see thousands of students each year and are familiar with all kinds of writing assignments and writing dilemmas.

Other Kinds of Resources

If you want feedback on a writing assignment and can't find a real live person to read it for you, there are other places to turn. These resources can give you tips for proofreading your own work, making an argument, using commas and transitions, and more. You can also try the spell/grammar checker on your computer. This shouldn't be your primary source of feedback, but it may be helpful.

A Word about Feedback and Plagiarism

Asking for help on your writing does not equal plagiarism, but talking with classmates about your work may feel like cheating. Check with your professor or TA about what kinds of help you can get legally.

Most will encourage you to discuss your ideas about the reading and lectures with your classmates. In general, if someone offers a particularly helpful insight, it makes sense to cite him or her in a footnote. The best way to avoid plagiarism is to write by yourself with your books closed.

What to do with the Feedback you Get

- Don't be intimidated if your professor or TA has written a lot on your paper. Sometimes instructors will provide more feedback on papers that they believe have a lot of potential. They may have written a lot because your ideas are interesting to them and they want to see you develop them to their fullest by improving your writing.
- By the same token, don't feel that your paper is garbage if the instructor didn't write much on it. Some graders just write more than others do, and sometimes your instructors are too busy to spend a great deal of time writing comments on each individual paper.
- If you receive feedback before the paper is due, think about what you can and can't do before the deadline. You sometimes have to triage your revisions. By all means, if you think you have major changes to make and you have time to make them, go for it.

  But if you have two other papers to write and all three are due tomorrow, you may have to decide that your thesis or your organization is the biggest issue and just focus on that. The paper might not be perfect, but you can learn from the experience for the next assignment.
- Read all of the feedback that you get. Many people, when receiving a paper back from their TA or professor, will just look at the grade and not read the comments written in

the margins or at the end of the paper. Even if you received a satisfactory grade, it makes sense to carefully read all of the feedback you get. Doing so may help you see patterns of error in your writing that you need to address and may help you improve your writing for future papers and for other classes.

- If you don't understand the feedback you receive, by all means ask the person who offered it. Feedback that you don't understand is feedback that you cannot benefit from, so ask for clarification when you need it.

  Remember that the person who gave you the feedback did so because they genuinely wanted to convey information to you that would help you become a better writer. They wouldn't want you to be confused and will be happy to explain their comments further if you ask.

- Ultimately, the paper you will turn in will be your own. You have the final responsibility for its form and content. Take the responsibility for being the final judge of what should and should not be done with your essay.

- Just because someone says to change something about your paper doesn't mean you should. Sometimes the person offering feedback can misunderstand your assignment or make a suggestion that doesn't seem to make sense. Don't follow those suggestions blindly. Talk about them, think about other options, and decide for yourself whether the advice you received was useful.

Final Thoughts

Finally, we would encourage you to think about feedback on your writing as a way to help you develop better writing strategies. This is the philosophy of the Writing Centre. Don't look at individual bits of feedback such as "This paper was badly organized" as evidence that you always organize ideas poorly. Think instead about the long haul. What writing process led you to a disorganized paper? What kinds of papers do you have organization problems with? What kinds of organization problems are they?

What kinds of feedback have you received about organization in the past? What can you do to resolve these issues, not just for one paper, but for all of your papers? The Writing Centre can help you with this process. Strategy-oriented thinking will help you go from being a writer who writes disorganized papers and then struggles to fix each one to being a writer who no longer writes disorganized papers. In the end, that's a much more positive and permanent solution.

Plagiarism

At University of North Carolina (UNC), plagiarism is defined as "the deliberate or reckless representation of another's words, thoughts, or ideas as one's own without attribution in connection with submission of academic work, whether graded or otherwise." Because it is considered a form of cheating, the Office of the Dean of Students can punish students who plagiarize with course failure and suspension.

Why are my Instructors so Concerned about Plagiarism?

In order to understand plagiarism, it helps to understand the process of sharing and creating ideas in the university. All knowledge is built from previous knowledge. As we read, study, perform experiments, and gather perspectives, we are using other people's ideas. Building on other people's ideas, we create our own. When you put your ideas on paper, your instructors want to distinguish between the building block ideas borrowed from other people and your own newly reasoned perspectives or conclusions. You make these distinctions in a written paper by citing the sources for your building block ideas. Giving clear credit for ideas matters in the professional community as well as in school.

Think of it this way: in the vast majority of assignments you'll get in college, your instructors will ask you to *read* something (think of this material as the building blocks) and then write a paper in which you *analyse* one or more aspects of what you have read (think of this as the new structure you build). Essentially, your instructors are asking you to do three things:

- Show that you have a clear understanding of the material you've read.
- Refer to your sources to support the ideas you have developed.
- Distinguish *your* analysis of what you've read from the author's analysis.

When you cite a source, you are using an expert's ideas as proof or evidence of a new idea that you are trying to communicate to the reader.

What about "Common Knowledge"?

In every professional field, experts consider some ideas "common knowledge," but remember that you're not a professional (yet). In fact, you're just learning about those concepts in the course you're taking, so the material you are reading may not yet be "common knowledge" to you. In order to decide if the material you want to use in your paper constitutes "common knowledge," you may find it helpful to ask yourself the following questions:

- Did I know this information before I took this course?
- Did this information/idea come from my own brain?

If you answer "no" to either or both of these questions, then the information is not "common knowledge" to you. In these cases, you need to cite your source(s) and indicate where you first learned this bit of what may be "common knowledge" in the field.

What about Paraphrasing?

Paraphrasing means taking another person's ideas and putting those ideas in your own words. Paraphrasing does not mean changing a word or two in someone else's sentence, changing the sentence structure while maintaining the original words, or changing a few words to synonyms.

If you are tempted to rearrange a sentence in any of these ways, you are writing too close to the original. That's plagiarizing, not paraphrasing.

Paraphrasing is a fine way to use another person's ideas to support your argument as long as you attribute the material to the author and cite the source in the text at the end of the sentence.

In order to make sure you are paraphrasing in the first place, take notes from your reading *with the book closed*. Doing so will make it easier to put the ideas in your own words. When you are unsure if you are writing too close to the original, check with your instructor before you turn in the paper for a grade.

How can I avoid Plagiarizing?

Now that you understand what plagiarism is, you're ready to employ the following three simple steps to avoid plagiarizing in your written work.

Step 1: Accentuate the Positive. Change your Attitude about Using Citations.

Do you feel that you use too many citations? Too few? Many students worry that if they use too many citations their instructors will think that they're relying too heavily on the source material and therefore not thinking for themselves.

In fact, however, using citations allows you to demonstrate clearly how well you understand the course material while *also* making clear distinctions between what the authors have to say and your analysis of their ideas.

Thus, rather than making your paper look less intellectually sophisticated, using citations allows you to show off your understanding of the material and the assignment. And instead of showing what you *don't* know, citing your sources provides evidence of what you *do* know and of the *authority* behind your knowledge.

Just make sure that your paper has a point, main idea, or thesis that is your own and that you organize the source material around that point.

Are you worried that you have too few citations? Double-check your assignment to see if you have been given any indication of the number or kind of source materials expected. Then share your writing with another reader.

Do you have enough evidence or proof to support the ideas you put forward? Why should the reader believe the points you have made? Would adding another, expert voice strengthen your argument? Who else agrees or disagrees with the ideas you have written? Have you paraphrased ideas that you have read or heard? If so, you need to cite them. Have you referred to or relied on course material to develop your ideas? If you, you need to cite it as well.

Step 2: How can I keep track of all this Information? Improve your Note-taking Skills.

Once you've reconsidered your position on using citations, you need to rethink your note-taking practices. Taking careful notes is simply the best way to avoid plagiarism. And improving your note-taking skills will also allow you to refine your critical thinking skills. Here's how the process works:

1. Start by carefully noting all the bibliographic information you'll need for your works cited page. If you're photocopying an article or section out of a book or journal, why not photocopy the front pages of the source as well?

   That way you'll have the bibliographic information if you need it later. If you forget to gather the information for a book, you can usually get it from the library's online card catalogue.

   Simply pull up the entry for the book you used to see the bibliographic information on that source. If you're working on an article from a journal, you can return to the database from which you got the original citation to find the bibliographic information.

2. Next, try thinking about your notes as a kind of transitional "space" between what you've read and what you're preparing to write. Imagine yourself having a conversation with the author of the story/novel/play/poem/article/book

you're reading, in which you repeatedly ask yourself the following questions:

- *What* is the author trying to explain?
- *Why* does she/he think these points are important?
- *How* has she/he decided to construct the argument?
- *How* does the structure of the argument affect the reader's response to the author's ideas?
- How *effective* is the author's argument?

Adopting this "conversational" approach to note-taking will improve your analysis of the material by leading you to notice not just what the author says, but also *how* and *why* the author communicates his or her ideas.

This strategy will also help you avoid the very common temptation of thinking that the author's way of explaining something is much better than anything you could write.

If you are tempted to borrow the author's language, write your notes *with the book closed* to ensure that you are putting the ideas into your own words. If you've already taken a step away from the author's words in your notes, you'll find it easier to use your own words in the paper you write.

3. Finally, be careful to use quotation marks to distinguish the exact words used by the author from your own words so that when you return to your notes later in the writing process, you won't have to guess which ideas are yours and which ones came directly from the text.

   You'll have to experiment with different note-taking techniques until you find the one that works best for you, but here's one example of how your notes might look:

Step 3: So many details, so little time! Locate the appropriate style manual.

Don't worry—no one can remember all the different citation conventions used in all the different university disciplines! Citing your sources appropriately is a matter of:

1. Determining which style your instructor wants you to use.
2. Finding the appropriate style manual, and
3. Copying the "formula" it gives for each type of source you use.

First, carefully read the assignment to determine what citation style your instructor wants you to use. If she/he doesn't specify a citation style in the assignment, check your syllabus, coursepack, and/or Blackboard site. If you can't find the citation style in any of those places, ask your instructor what style she/he prefers.

Second, academic citation styles follow specific formats, so making an educated guess about how to structure your citations and works cited page is usually not a good idea. Instead, find the specified style manual in the reference section of the library, on the reference shelf in the Writing Centre, or online.

Finally, style manuals provide easy-to-follow formulas for your citations. For example, the MLA handbook provides the following format for citing a book by a single author:

Author's name. *Title of the book*. Publication information.

You can use this formula for your own citation by simply plugging in the information called for, following the format of the formula itself. Here's an example of how that might look:

Sinha, Rashmi. ***Effective Editing*. Lotus Press Publishers and Distributors 2011.**

How can I tell Whether I've Plagiarized?

If you've followed the above guidelines but still aren't sure whether you've plagiarized, you can double-check your work using the checklist below.

You need to cite your source, even if:

1. You put all direct quotes in quotation marks.
2. You changed the words used by the author into synonyms.
3. You completely paraphrased the ideas to which you referred.
4. Your sentence is mostly made up of your own thoughts, but contains a reference to the author's ideas.

■■■

CHAPTER 7

Effective Editing

Editing Principles

- **Build on Strength**—Identify what you think is working well and carry it through the rest of the text.
- **Cut What Can Be Cut**—Everything in the text must realte to the single dominant meaning of the text. If it doesn't, it should go!
- **Simplicity is Best**—The writing should be as simple as possible; write so your readers understand what you want them to.
- **Listen to the Writing** —Your ear is a better editor than your eye. Read aloud. The piece will tell you when it needs a definition woven in, some additional clarification, more evidence, a change of pace.

Checklist for a "First" Read

Reading for Meaning

Read the text fast—find a comfortable chair, put your pencil down, read as if you are a naive reader; try not to get too close to the text; instead, aim for a sense of the overall meaning.

- Can you write a short (a sentence or two) synopsis of what the piece is about?
- Do readers need more information?
- Is the piece too long? Is it too short?
- Does it go off on tangents that can be cut?
- Are there elements that should be cut, or developed more fully?
- Are readers' key questions answered?
- Does the piece deliver on the promise made in the title and lede?
- Is there scaffolding that was useful in shaping the piece but can now be cut?

Now pick up a pencil and make marginal notes—think about your overall meaning.

Checklist for a "Second" Read

Reading for Order

Continue reading at a good clip. Don't stop for language problems—that will come later. Now you're dealing with chunks to make sure each section is developed well and is in the right place.

- Is the title on target?
- Does the lede establish the voice for the piece?
- Does the draft "show" as well as "tell"?
- Is each section an answer to readers' questions?

- Is each piece of documentation appropriate for the point being made?
- Does the pace keep readers moving but allow time to absorb your argument?
- Does the end echo the lede and give readers a sense of completion?
- Does the argument follow logically?
- Have you tried rearranging elements?

Checklist for a "Third" Read

Proofreading or Reading for Voice, Language, and Conventions

It's time to get out your sharpest pencil and be ruthless. It's generally useful to do a "third" read with hard copy in front of you, where you can make actual marks on the paper. It's do-able on a screen but you're more likely to miss stuff you'd see if you were working on a printout.

- Are inportant pieces of specific information at the ends and beginnings of key sentences, paragraphs, sections, and the entire piece itself?
- Have you used "subject-verb-object" sentences?
- Have you cut unnecessary clauses?
- Are there sentences that announce what you're going to say, or sum up what you've already said—can you cut them?
- Do readers leave each sentence with more information than when they began?
- Is sentence length varied, with shorter sentences usually used for clarification or emphasis?

- Is each word the right word?
- Is each word the simplest word?
- Have you used strong verbs?
- Have unnecessary adverbs and adjectives been eliminated?
- Have you cut "to be" verbs wherever possible?
- Have you eliminated "-ings" wherever possible?
- Have you used active voice?
- Is the simplest tense used?
- Are tenses consistent?
- What about pronoun agreement?
- Have you checked for parallel structure?
- Have you checked for gender-biased or racist language?
- Have you cut unnecessary words: that, would, quite, very...
- Have sentence elements been reorderred so they read naturally and smoothly?
- Have you used parallel structure in lists?
- Does each paragraph make one point?
- Have you developed that point fully?
- Do paragraphs vary in length, with shorter paragraphs used for clarification and emphasis?
- Are the paragraphs in order, do transitions make sense?
- Have you cut unnecessary introductory and concluding paragraphs?
- Can you think of questions readers might still ask?

- Have you checked punctuation?
- Have you checked spelling?
- Are the numbers correct?

Tips for Doing a "Third" Read

- Read backwards. Begin at the end and work back through the text paragraph by paragraph or even line by line.

  This will force you to look at the surface elements rather than the meaning of the text.
- Place a ruler under each line as you read it. This will give your eyes a manageable amount of text to read.
- Know your own typical mistakes. Keep a running list of errors you typically make. Before you do a "third" read, look over your list.
- Read for one type of error at a time. If commas are your most frequent problem, go through the writing checking just that one problem.

  Then read again for the next most frequent problem.
- Read through your writing several times fast, once looking just at spelling, another time looking just at punctuation, and so on.

  This will help you focus so you'll do a better job.

Correctness: Spelling, Punctuation, Grammar, and Style

Spelling, punctuation, grammar, and style are often the primary concern of many writers—that's a holdover from school days where teachers emphasized "correctness".

In actual fact, a writer's first concern should be **fluency**—developing the ideas of any piece of writing.

The second concern then becomes **clarity**—making the writing make sense to others.

Finally comes **correctness**—making the text conform to the conventions of standard written English.

In other words, the developmental sequence for any piece of writing ought to be:

- fluency
- clarity
- correctness

These three dimensions, of course, continually overlap; even experienced writers can have problems with fluency—particularly when writing on a new topic or in a new genre.

Under those circumstances, focusing on correctness won't help with the problem; what you have to do is focus on invention and shaping ideas.

Once you have your ideas sorted out, the writing more or less clear, it does become appropriate, even mandatory, to think about the conventions of standard written English—to proofread to make sure spelling is correct, that grammar is conventional, that punctuation aids in making meaning, that word usage (or style) is acceptable.

There are a ton of resources online to assist you with spelling, punctuation, grammar, and style. One of the most comprehensive is:

- **Online Writing Lab (Purdue University)** for information about these topics.

- **Resources for Business and Technical Writers** for further helpful resources.

Online Quizzes

Are you sure you have a handle on spelling, punctuation, and grammar? Try the online quizzes below! Some of them are quite challenging. Answers are provided for all of them, explanations are provided with some.

- Common Usage Errors
- Common Spelling Errors
- Commonly Confused Word Pairs
- Subject Verb Agreement
- Active/Passive Voice
- Commonly Misspelled Words
- Sentence Fragments
- Run-on Sentences
- Comma Splices
- Using Commas
- Apostrophes
- Quotation Marks
- Punctuation
- Commas *vs* Semicolons
- Verb Tense Consistency

Writing Fast

Writing fast is about uninhibited invention and good organization.

- Allow yourself to start anywhere; you don't have to start at the beginning.
- Move to some other aspect of the topic if you find yourself bogged down.
- Let digressions happen; they may prove fruitful later.
- Don't try getting it right the first time—draft / rewrite as many times as you need to make the writing clear.
- Write down thoughts when they strike you even if you're doing something else.
- Keep a separate "thoughts" file.
- Try talking your thoughts out loud.
- Write about your frustrations.
- False starts and dead ends are normal; just pick up somewhere else.
- Be willing to throw stuff away.
- You have a reasonably good idea of what you want to write—then make an outline.
- Don't let yourself be trapped by your outline; abandon it if you find it draining your energy.
- Don't edit or proofread before you have a complete draft.
- You can save time by putting in a placeholder and filling in a section later.
- You don't need to wait until you've "completed" your "research" before you begin—research will still be necessary while you're drafting, rewriting, editing and even proofing!
- Allow yourself to be messy—spread paper all over your

desk and floor; scribble, use arrows all over your printouts.

- Talk out your ideas to someone else.
- Just write and keep writing.
- Make lists.
- Use highlighters.
- Always create a separate "references" file; fully record each reference (including page numbers) as soon as you've cited it in your writing.
- Save **all** deleted sections to an out-takes file; that material might be useful.
- Brainstorm on index cards—they're easy to move around.
- Don't worry about order in your writing—you'll shift elements around later.
- Use point form; it forces you to be succinct and it's easy to flesh out.
- Revisit your thoughts file—there may be ideas there to strengthen what you've written.
- While you're inventing/drafting: If in doubt—**PUT IT IN!**
- During rewriting: If in doubt—**TAKE IT OUT!**
- Be sure to leave enough time to do a careful "third" read.
- Solicit feedback from naive readers and from experts.
- Develop an outline after you're finished; this lets you check the architecture of your piece.

- Introductions are often best left to last! It's not until you're finished that you really know what the piece is about.
- Remember, no part is done until the whole is done! Don't "finish" one part before working on another—the parts need to interact.
- Set yourself deadlines.

Procedural Blocks

- We can be in the position of not knowing what to write next.

  At a global level we know and can specify clearly what we want to write about, and we have no trouble putting one word after another—we're lost in between—perhaps in deciding precisely what we want in the next paragraph.
- Procedural blocks are particularly acute at the beginning—the problem arises because we can visualize a set of alternatives without obvious reason for selecting any particular one.
- There are several reasons for procedural blocks.
    - Trying to pack too much information into a sentence, a paragraph, leaving too many directions to follow at once.
    - Digressions which we've been led into by our developing ideas.
    - Our proliferating intentions getting ahead of us.
    - Crossing into a new section of the writing.

Psychological Blocks

- We can't let words come—the most difficult moment with

any piece of writing is at the beginning when the first words should come.

- It's not a matter of having no words, but we can't bring ourselves to let them appear on paper or screen.
- There are three major reasons for not being able to write:
    - The magnitude of the task seems overwhelming.
    - Anxiety regarding our fears that what we produce won't be good enough.
    - Being afraid we don't have anything worthwhile to say—being reluctant to write anything.

Strategies for Overcoming Blocks

- **Write!**
- Write anything, no matter how irrelevant you think it is.
- If in doubt, **PUT IT IN!**
- Open a new file and experiment.
- Too many directions at once?

  List them and flesh each one out (brainstorm, make lists...)
- Don't have a beginning?

  Start somewhere else.
- Can't get what you want to say next from what you've just written?

  Write what you want to say anyway (later you'll figure out how to handle the transition).
- Not sure how to shape the next part?

  Try a couple of alternatives.
- Don't have the next bit sufficiently clear in your head?

Take a walk, cook a meal, watch TV, sleep on it...

Our brain doesn't solve problems under pressure, give yourself incubation time.

- Can't pick up from where you left off?

  Begin rewriting the last paragraph, or just start somewhere else.

- Avoiding a particular writing project by answering mail?

  Stop procrastinating and make yourself write on the task you're avoiding.

- **Don't Expect writing to Come out Right the First Time**

  Anything you write can be thrown away (or put in an "out-takes" file for later rescue if necessary)

- Deadlines help!

  Set a time for completing a particular writing assignment.

- **Writing blocks are resolved ONLY by writing!**

The Reading Process

Reading is a complex constructive process involving both **visual** and **non-visual** information—what's in front of the eyes and what's behind them. The essential skill all competent readers learn is to depend on their eyes as little as possible.

Of course, your eyes have a role to play in reading, but visual information is not enough in itself.

You bring to any encounter with written text your understanding of the particular language a text is written in, both word meanings and its grammatical structure, as well as as your familiarity with the subject-matter, your experience with reading, and especially what you know about reading different kinds of writing.

Because reading is inherently dependent on what readers know, there can be no "literal" meaning of any text—there will be as many meanings as there are readers; no one of them is literal.

When a group of readers has common knowledge, their interpretations of a particular text will converge, but there is no guarantee that all readers will construct the same meaning.

Interpretive Community

What's important for technical writers to judge is the breadth of knowledge about the subject their readers are likely to have. If the audience is large, it's unrealistic to expect all of your readers to come to your text with the same background. Realize there are likely to be gaps; do your best to anticipate them.

What works in your favour is the interpretive community—the potential shared meaning of a group of professional readers. Your sense of what your interpretive community is likely to know allows you to make some assumptions as you write.

But remember, there is no guarantee any particular reader shares your interpretive community. There is no way you can write a text that makes a particular interpretation a certainty! So try out your writing on both naive and expert readers.

Intertextuality

What's in any particular text itself can only hint at the inferential meaning a reader is invited to make. To participate fully in reading any text requires a sense of **intertextuality**. Readers relate the current piece they're reading to other texts they've read on the same subject, as well as connecting information from things they've read on related subjects.

Readers must be familiar in advance not only with the general content, but have some particular background knowledge of the specific domain of the text.

This is a key aspect of the transactional nature of reading along with technical, cultural, and linguistic contexts and the more widely read the audience, the more likely they will make sense of your writing—although not necessarily the sense you intend them to make.

To the extent that the writer and reader share such contexts, there will be convergence of interpretation. Texts are not transparent; they don't directly reveal their meaning.

Readers construct meaning based on a large number of factors. Writers have to remember reading is a process of making inferences.

Responding to Writers

All writers experience trepidation when they contemplate showing their writing to someone else! That's a by-product of what happened to your writing in school—your teachers told you what they thought were the weak and strong points and suggested things you should change.

However, to improve your writing you don't need advice about what changes to make. You don't need theories of what is good and bad writing.

What you need to know is what sense your readers have

made, what questions they have, where they got confused, what digressions they took off on when they read your words. You need what Peter Elbow calls "movies of people's minds".

Here are some suggestions for giving **movies of your mind** when reading for another writer. This is the same feedback you'll find helpful from your readers, as well.

- Start by simply pointing to the words and phrases which stood out for you, either because they seemed particularly apt or because they were jarring for some reason.
- Summarize the writing:
    - Tell quickly what you thought were the main points, the center of gravity of the piece.
    - See if you can summarize the whole thing in a single sentence.
    - Don't plan or think too much about it; the point is to help the writer see what stood out in your head—it's not a test to see if you got the meaning "right"!
- Tell the writer everything that happened to you when you read the writing—it's useful to tell it as a story: "I felt confused about ..., but then I saw a connection.... I especially liked... I found myself going back after ..."

The important thing in telling is not to get too far away from talking about the actual writing; remember the writer is interested in how his or her writing worked.

- When you read something you have perceptions and reactions that you're not fully aware of and therefore can't "tell" about. However, you may be able to show them:

  - Talk about the writing as if you were describing voices: it lectured, it droned, it ran…
  - Talk about the writing as if you were talking about weather: it was foggy, clear, crisp…
  - Talk about the writing as if you were talking about motion: it marched, strolled…
  - Describe what you think the writer's intentions were
  - Writing is like a lump of clay—tell what you'd do with that clay.
  - Paint the picture the writing conjured up for you.
- Try writing a quick synopsis and share it with the writer.

Telling is like looking inside yourself to see what you can report; showing is like installing a window in the top of your head so the writer can see for him or herself.

Some General Advice to Readers

- Make sure you've had enough time to read the piece through twice, taking a bit of time between each reading to let the words and ideas sink in. Don't let yourself be hurried.
- Remember no kind of reaction is wrong, insufficient, perhaps, but not wrong. So don't struggle with your reactions—just let them happen.
- Try to avoid giving advice; on the other hand, if the interaction between you and the words produces some suggestions, don't hold back.
- Like advice, evaluation in itself has no value; it doesn't provide insight into your experience as a reader.
- Your job as reader is to offer the writer your immediate impressions; you're not trying to fix the writing but to help the writer understand your experience of it.

Some General Advice to Writers

- Be quite and listen!
- After you have a reader's reactions you can explain what you intended or what you think you've put into the writing.
- Don't reject what readers tell you—listen to what they say as if it were all true. You can consider their responses later.
- Listen openly and take it in, but don't be paralyzed by what they tell you.
- You're not looking for readers to tell you how to write; you need them to tell you what thought processes your writing evoked.
- Remember, it's their job to give you their experience; it's your job to decide what to do with that information—you don't have to act on any response, you just have to consider what it tells you about your writing.

Make sure your readers know what you want from them—spell it out. If there's some particular kind of feedback you would find helpful, ask for it.

■■■

Chapter 8

Proofreading

Proofreading is the final stage of the editing process, focusing on surface errors such as misspellings and mistakes in grammar and punctuation. You should proofread only after you have finished all of your other editing revisions.

Teachers, business people, and just about everyone else it seems complain often and loudly that people today (usually "kids today") don't know how to write. I'm convinced, though, that a big part of the problem (perhaps the *biggest* part of the problem) is that people don't know how to *edit*. We labour under the notion that good writing flows easily from the pen or typing fingers, and that editing too much will "kill" our work.

The best writers know differently, of course—their memoirs and biographies and writing manuals are filled with stories of books that needed to be cut in half to be readable, sentences that took weeks or months to get just right, and lifetimes spent tinkering with a single work that never strikes them as "just right". To paraphrase a common saying among writers, **there is no good writing, only good re-writing**.

But if writing isn't taught well enough or often enough these days, editing is hardly taught at all. This is too bad, since **editing is where the real work of writing is at**.

More than just proofreading, **good editing improves the clarity and forcefulness of a piece**. Here's some tips and tricks to help you make your writing more effective:

- **Read out loud:** Reading a piece out loud helps you to identify clunky, awkward passages that seem to make sense to the eye, especially to the author's eye.
- **Read in reverse:** You may have heard about reading backwards, word by word, to help proofread. This works because you bypass your brain's tendency to fill in what it expects to see, allowing you to catch spelling errors you might otherwise gloss over.

  This is useless, though, when it comes to content, where meaning comes from phrases and word order. Instead, read from back to front, sentence by sentence (or maybe paragraph by paragraph, or both) to make sure that each sentence and each paragraph is internally coherent — that it makes sense on its own.
- **Sleep on it:** Wait at least a night, and preferably longer, before starting your editing. Ideally, you want to forget what you wrote, so that — again — your brain doesn't see what it expects to see but only sees what's really there.

  A lot of times we make logical errors that make sense at the time, because our minds are filled with ideas, examples, and arguments related to our topic; when we approach our writing with a clear mind, though, those mental connections are gone, and only what we've actually written counts.

- **Cut, don't add:** We are almost always too wordy. While you may need to add a word or two while editing, for the most part you should be removing words. Concise writing is more powerful and easier to read than lengthy prose.
- **Justify yourself:** Every point, statement, question, joke, even every word should have a reason to be in your piece; if it doesn't, strike it. Be harsh — if a word or phrase does not add value to your writing, get rid of it.
- **Establish cognizance of pretentious language usages and eliminate such material:** That is, watch for fancy words and cut them. Inexperienced writers often ape the language of academia, or rather the language they imagine academia uses. Even if you're *in* academia, don't use academic writing as a model.

  While there is a time and place for jargon, for the most part jargon exists to exclude readers, not include them. For most readers, the language of journalists is a much more appropriate model — and that means aiming for at best a smart eighth-grader's reading level.
- **Throw out and get rid of unnecessary redundancies you don't need:** This applies in both sentences and the work as a whole. In high school, you might have learned to "say it, say it again, and then say what you said"; for most readers, this is a waste of their time and an insult to their intelligence; in the end, they'll just tune you out. Say it clearly the first time, then move on.
- **Kill unsightly adverbs:** Some adverbs are fine, but usually they serve only to pad out a statement that doesn't need padding. For example: "He ran quickly". It is in the nature

of running to be quick. If there's something unusual about his running (perhaps he ran *slowly*), then mention it; if not, just say "he ran" and trust your readers to know what running means.

- **Passive sentences are to be avoided:** Beware of the use of "to be" and its conjugations (is, was, were, are, am). These often indicate a passive sentence, where the subject is acted upon instead of acting. Passivity makes for weak, unconvincing writing.

  Passivity is often the hallmark of someone trying to weasel out of something: "Mistakes were made" assigns no blame, while "I made a mistake" tells the world you're taking responsibility. It does not convey the action, it only suggests the effect. So avoid passive sentences.

Good editing, like good writing (or, better, *as part of* good writing), is an art. **It takes time and practice to develop a real talent for editing, but the end result is worth it — your writing will be more alive, more effective, and ultimately more likely to be read.** And that is, after all, what's important: that your audience reads and, just as crucially, understands your work

Why Proofread? It's the content that really matters, Right?

Content is important. But like it or not, the way a paper looks affects the way others judge it. When you've worked hard to develop and present your ideas, you don't want careless errors distracting your reader from what you have to say. It's worth paying attention to the details that help you to make a good impression.

Most people devote only a few minutes to proofreading,

hoping to catch any glaring errors that jump out from the page. But a quick and cursory reading, especially after you've been working long and hard on a paper, usually misses a lot. It's better to work with a definite plan that helps you to search systematically for specific kinds of errors.

Sure, this takes a little extra time, but it pays off in the end. If you know that you have an effective way to catch errors when the paper is almost finished, you can worry less about editing while you are writing your first drafts. This makes the entire writing proccess more efficient.

Try to keep the editing and proofreading processes separate. When you are editing an early draft, you don't want to be bothered with thinking about punctuation, grammar, and spelling. If your worrying about the spelling of a word or the placement of a comma, you're not focusing on the more important task of developing and connecting ideas.

The Proofreading Process

You probably already use some of the strategies discussed below. Experiment with different tactics until you find a system that works well for you. The important thing is to make the process systematic and focused so that you catch as many errors as possible in the least amount of time.

- *Don't rely entirely on spelling checkers.* These can be useful tools but they are far from foolproof. Spell checkers have a limited dictionary, so some words that show up as misspelled may really just not be in their memory. In addition, spell checkers will not catch misspellings that form another valid word. For example, if you type "your" instead of "you're," "to" instead of "too," or "there" instead of "their," the spell checker won't catch the error.

- *Grammar checkers can be even more problematic.* These programmes work with a limited number of rules, so they can't identify every error and often make mistakes. They also fail to give thorough explanations to help you understand why a sentence should be revised.

  You may want to use a grammar checker to help you identify potential run-on sentences or too-frequent use of the passive voice, but you need to be able to evaluate the feedback it provides.

- *Proofread for only one kind of error at a time.* If you try to identify and revise too many things at once, you risk losing focus, and your proofreading will be less effective. It's easier to catch grammar errors if you aren't checking punctuation and spelling at the same time. In addition, some of the techniques that work well for spotting one kind of mistake won't catch others.

- *Read slow, and read every word.* Try reading out loud, which forces you to say each word and also lets you hear how the words sound together. When you read silently or too quickly, you may skip over errors or make unconscious corrections.

- *Separate the text into individual sentences.* This is another technique to help you to read every sentence carefully. Simply press the return key after every period so that every line begins a new sentence.

  Then read each sentence separately, looking for grammar, punctuation, or spelling errors. If you're working with a printed copy, try using an opaque object like a ruler or a piece of paper to isolate the line you're working on.

- *Circle every punctuation mark.* This forces you to look at each one. As you circle, ask yourself if the punctuation is correct.

- *Read the paper backwards.* This technique is helpful for checking spelling. Start with the last word on the last page and work your way back to the beginning, reading each word separately.

  Because content, punctuation, and grammar won't make any sense, your focus will be entirely on the spelling of each word. You can also read backwards sentence by sentence to check grammar; this will help you avoid becoming distracted by content issues.

- *Proofreading is a learning process.* You're not just looking for errors that you recognize; you're also learning to recognize and correct new errors. This is where handbooks and dictionaries come in. Keep the ones you find helpful close at hand as you proofread.

- *Ignorance may be bliss, but it won't make you a better proofreader.* You'll often find things that don't seem quite right to you, but you may not be quite sure what's wrong either. A word looks like it might be misspelled, but the spell checker didn't catch it.

  You think you need a comma between two words, but you're not sure why. Should you use "that" instead of "which"? If you're not sure about something, look it up.

- *The proofreading process becomes more efficient as you develop and practice a systematic strategy.* You'll learn to identify the specific areas of your own writing that need careful attention, and knowing that you have a sound method for finding errors will help you to focus more on developing your ideas while you are drafting the paper.

General Tips for Proofreading

- Read it out loud and also silently.
- Read it backwards to focus on the spelling of words.
- Read it upside down to focus on typology.
- Use a spell checker and grammar checker as a first screening, but don't depend on them.
- Have others read it.
- Read it slowly.
- Use a screen (a blank sheet of paper to cover the material not yet proofed).
- Point with your finger to read one word at a time.
- Don't proof for every type of mistake at once—do one proof for spelling, another for missing/additional spaces, consistency of word usage, font sizes, etc.
- Keep a list of your most common errors (or of the writers you are proofing) and proof for those on separate "trips."
- If you are editing within Word, use the "track changes" or "mark changes" function to make your comments apparent to other reviewers (additions and deletions can be set to appear in different colours).
- Print it out and read it.
- Read down columns in a table, even if you're supposed to read across the table to use the information. Columns may be easier to deal with than rows.
- Use editor's flags. Put # in the document where reviewers need to pay special attention, or next to items that need to be double-checked before the final proof print. Do a final search for all # flags and remove them.

- Give a copy of the document to another person and keep a copy yourself. Take turns reading it out loud to each other. While one of you reads, the other one follows along to catch any errors and awkward-sounding phrases. This method also works well when proofing numbers and codes.
- First, proof the body of the text. Then go back and proof the headings. Headings are prone to error because copy editors often don't focus on them.
- Double check fonts that are unusual (italic, bold, or otherwise different).
- Carefully read type in very tiny font.
- Be careful that your eyes don't skip from one error to the next obvious error, missing subtle errors in between.
- Double check proper names.
- Double check little words: "or," "of," "it," and "is" are often interchanged.
- Double check boilerplate text, like the company letterhead. Just because it's frequently used doesn't mean it's been carefully checked.
- Double check whenever you're sure something is right—certainty is dangerous.
- Closely review page numbers and other footer/header material for accuracy and correct order.

Editing for Content

- Ask yourself who, what, when, where, why, and how when reading for content. Does the text answer all the questions you think it should?

- Highlight the sentences that best answer these questions, just so you can see if the facts flow in logical order.
- Do the math, do the math, and then do the math again. Somewhere between the screen and the printer 2+2 often becomes 3.
- Make a list of "bugaboo" words and do a search for them before final proof. Include every swear word, words related to product terminology, and other words that pop up on occasion. Then do a "find" for all these words.
- Actually do every step in procedures to make sure they are complete, accurate, and in correct order.
- Count the number of steps a list promises to make sure they are all there.
- Check that figure numbers match their references in the text and are sequential.
- Check that illustrations, pictographs, and models are right-side up.

Preparing yourself to Proof or Edit

- Write at the end of the day; edit first thing in the morning. (Usually, getting some sleep in between helps.)
- Listen to music or chew gum. Proofing can be boring business and it doesn't require much critical thinking, though it does require extreme focus and concentration. Anything that can relieve your mind of some of the pressure, while allowing you to still keep focused, is a benefit.
- Don't use fluorescent lighting when proofing. The flicker rate is actually slower than standard lighting. Your eyes can't pick up inconsistencies as easily under fluorescent lighting.

- Spend an half-hour a month reviewing grammar rules.
- Read something else between edits. This helps clear your head of what you expect to read and allows you to read what really is on the page.
- Make a list of things to watch for—a kind of "to do" list—as you edit.

Is Editing the same thing as Proofreading?

Not exactly. Although many people use the terms interchangeably, editing and proofreading are two different stages of the revision process. Both demand close and careful reading, but they focus on different aspects of the writing and employ different techniques.

Some tips that apply to both Editing and Proofreading

- *Get some distance from the text!* It's hard to edit or proofread a paper that you've just finished writing—it's still to familiar, and you tend to skip over a lot of errors. Put the paper aside for a few hours, days, or weeks. Go for a run. Take a trip to the beach.

  Clear your head of what you've written so you can take a fresh look at the paper and see what is really on the page. Better yet, give the paper to a friend—you can't get much more distance than that. Someone who is reading the paper for the first time, comes to it with completely fresh eyes.
- *Decide what medium lets you proofread most carefully.* Some people like to work right at the computer, while others like to sit back with a printed copy that they can mark up as they read.

- *Try changing the look of your document.* Altering the size, spacing, color, or style of the text may trick your brain into thinking it's seeing an unfamiliar document, and that can help you get a different perspective on what you've written.
- *Find a quiet place to work.* Don't try to do your proofreading in front of the TV or while you're chugging away on the treadmill. Find a place where you can concentrate and avoid distractions.
- *If possible, do your editing and proofreading in several short blocks of time,* rather than all at once—otherwise, your concentration is likely to wane.
- *If you're short on time, you may wish to prioritize* your editing and proofreading tasks to be sure that the most important ones are completed.

Editing

Editing is what you begin doing as soon as you finish your first draft. You reread your draft to see, for example, whether the paper is well-organized, the transitions between paragraphs are smooth, and your evidence really backs up your argument. You can edit on several levels:

Content

Have you done everything the assignment requires? Are the claims you make accurate? If it is required to do so, does your paper make an argument? Is the argument complete? Are all of your claims consistent? Have you supported each point with adequate evidence? Is all of the information in your paper relevant to the assignment and/or your overall writing goal?

Overall Structure

Does your paper have an appropriate introduction and conclusion? Is your thesis clearly stated in your introduction? Is it clear how each paragraph in the body of your paper is related to your thesis? Are the paragraphs arranged in a logical sequence? Have you made clear transitions between paragraphs? One way to check the structure of your paper is to make an outline of the paper after you have written the first draft.

Structure within Paragraphs

Does each paragraph have a clear topic sentence? Does each paragraph stick to one main idea? Are there any extraneous or missing sentences in any of your paragraphs?

Clarity

Have you defined any important terms that might be unclear to your reader? Is the meaning of each sentence clear? (One way to answer this question is to read your paper one sentence at a time, starting at the end and working backwards so that you will not unconsciously fill in content from previous sentences.)

Is it clear what each pronoun (he, she, it, they, which, who, this, etc.) refers to? Have you chosen the proper words to express your ideas? Avoid using words you find in the thesaurus that aren't part of your normal vocabulary; you may misuse them.

Style

Have you used an appropriate tone (formal, informal, persuasive, etc.)? Is your use of gendered language (masculine and feminine pronouns like "he" or "she," words like "fireman" that contain "man," and words that some people incorrectly assume apply to only one gender—for example, some people assume "nurse" must refer to a woman) appropriate? Have you varied the length and structure of your sentences? Do you tends to use the passive voice too often? Does your writing contain a lot of unnecessary phrases like "there is," "there are," "due to the fact that," etc.? Do you repeat a strong word (for example, a vivid main verb) unnecessarily?

Citations

Have you appropriately cited quotes, paraphrases, and ideas you got from sources? Are your citations in the correct format?

As you edit at all of these levels, you will usually make significant revisions to the content and wording of your paper. Keep an eye out for patterns of error; knowing what kinds of problems you tend to have will be helpful, especially if you are editing a large document like a thesis or dissertation.

Once you have identified a pattern, you can develop techniques for spotting and correcting future instances of that pattern. For example, if you notice that you often discuss several distinct topics in each paragraph, you can go through your paper and underline the key words in each paragraph, then break the paragraphs up so that each one focuses on just one main idea.

■■■

Chapter 9

Copyediting

Copyediting, also written as ***copy-editing*** or ***copyediting***, is the work that an editor does to improve the formatting, style, and accuracy of text. Unlike general editing, copyediting often does not involve changing the substance of the text. *Copy* refers to written or typewritten text for typesetting, printing, or publication. Copyediting is done before proofreading, which is the last step in the editorial cycle.

In some countries an editor who does this work is called a ***copy editor***, and an organization's highest-ranking copy editor, or the supervising editor of a group of copy editors, may be known as the ***copy chief***, *copy desk chief*, or *news editor*.

In book publishing in the United Kingdom and other parts of the world that follow UK nomenclature, the term *copy editor* is used, but in newspaper and magazine publishing, the term is ***sub-editor***, commonly shortened to *sub* (*to sub* is the verb form). The senior sub-editor on a title is called the *chief sub-editor*. As the "sub" prefix suggests, copy editors typically have less authority than regular editors.

The alternate spellings ***copyedit*** and ***copy-edit*** are fairly common. Similarly, the term *copy editor* may also be spelled as one word or in hyphenated form. The hyphenated form is especially common in the UK. In the U.S. newspaper field, using two words is more common.

The "five Cs" summarize the copy editor's job: Make the copy clear, correct, concise, comprehensible, and consistent. Copy editors should *Make it say what it means, and mean what it says*.

Typically, copy editing involves correcting spelling, punctuation, grammar, terminology and jargon, timelines, and semantics; ensuring that the typescript adheres to the publisher's style. Often, copy editors are also responsible for adding any "display copy", such as headlines, standardized headers and footers, and photo captions.

Copy editors are expected to ensure that the text flows, that it is sensible, fair, and accurate, and that any legal problems have been addressed. Some newspaper copy editors select stories from wire service copy.

Copy editors may shorten the text, to improve it or to fit length limits. This is particularly so in periodical publishing, where copy must be cut to fit the layout, and the text changed to ensure there are no 'short lines'.

Newspaper copy editors are considered the newspaper's last line of defense. Sometimes, the copy editor is the only person, other than the writer, to read an entire text before publication.

Copyediting is an important intermediary stage between acceptance and publication. Serving both the publisher and the author, the copyeditor's responsibilities embrace style and mechanics in addition to other aspects of the manuscript.

As Claire Kehrwald Cook notes in her book *Line by Line: How to Edit Your Own Writing,* a principal task of copyediting is to eliminate "the stylistic faults" that "impede reading and obscure meaning". Copyeditors concern themselves with questions of grammar, usage, and punctuation as well as with the correctness and consistency of other mechanical matters, such as spelling, capitalization, the treatment of numbers and names, and the documentation of scholarship. This aspect of copyediting frequently centers on making the manuscript conform to the house style the journal or press follows.

The copyeditor enables the publisher to ensure consistency in spelling, capitalization, italicization, and the like within a work and from one work to another. The copyeditor also marks up the manuscript for typesetting, specifying such design features as title, subheadings, set-down quotations, notes, and list of works cited. Besides stylistic and mechanical questions, the copyeditor may call attention to more-substantive matters that may not have been detected by the consultant readers and the acquisitions editor, such as errors of fact or logic, possibly unjustified generalizations, or even potential legal problems in the manuscript.

The successful copyeditor, therefore, routinely renders a manuscript more cogent and accessible to its readers and sometimes saves the author and the publisher from various kinds of professional discomfiture. Copyediting may be done on the paper or the electronic version of the manuscript. When working on hard copy, editors use a set of symbols to indicate changes-deletions, insertions, transpositions, and so forth- in the manuscript. Frequently the symbols are supplemented by explanations or clarifications in the margins or on slips attached to the page. Copyeditors also commonly use margins or slips to address queries to the author, requesting information or explication, for example, or suggesting alternative choices of wording. A copyeditor who works on computer usually produces at the end a new printout incorporating the editorial changes, which are often highlighted to allow the author to compare the original and copyedited versions more easily. Queries to the author are likely to appear not in the margins but elsewhere–for instance, all queries may be collected in a list keyed to numbers embedded in the text.

In returning the copyedited manuscript to the author for review, the editor usually sends a cover letter that, among other things, may call attention to special problems or give instructions about responding to changes and queries. The letter also normally specifies a deadline for the return of the manuscript. If you cannot meet the deadline, notify the editor immediately. Otherwise, the publisher will expect to receive the reviewed manuscript within the time requested, so that production can proceed on schedule. If no schedule is set, return the manuscript as quickly as possible.

When you receive a copyedited manuscript from your publisher, read the cover letter first, especially noting the deadline for return. Evaluate each suggested change and either accept the change or explain what is wrong with it and, if the copyeditor has identified a problem, substitute a different revision. If you do not understand a change, ask for clarification. If the copyediting was done on paper, do not erase or otherwise obliterate any change or query. Try to respond unambiguously and as near as possible on the page to the query; if space is insufficient, place replies on a separate sheet, making evident the pages and lines involved. For works destined for print publication, the review of the copyedited manuscript is normally the author's last chance to make revisions, such as correcting or updating references, for from this time forward, changes become costly (and are often charged to the author or not even made). If your revisions are brief, insert them within the manuscript; when lengthy or likely to lead to confusion if placed directly on the manuscript, revisions should be written on separate pages with clear indications of *where they* belong in the text.

Before returning the copyedited manuscript to the publisher, make sure you have answered all questions, supplied all requested information, and made all needed changes.

Besides meeting the deadline, follow any special instructions the publisher gives for the return of the manuscript. Include a cover letter explaining what you have carried out and noting any specific problems or questions of which the copyeditor should be aware.

If problems remain unresolved, the copyeditor may return to you with fur ther queries. For a text copyedited on computer, the editor normally transfers all final changes to the disk or disks containing the work. (Less frequently, some publishers ask authors to make the changes and to submit the final version on disk for composition.)

Changes in the Field

Traditionally, the copyeditor would read a printed or written manuscript, manually marking it with editor's correction marks. Today, the manuscript is more often read on a computer display and corrections are entered directly.

The rise of desktop publishing means that many copy editors do design and layout work that once was the province of design production crews in print publications. As a result, the skills needed for editing copy have shifted: Technical knowledge is sometimes considered as important as writing ability, though this is more true in journalism than it is in book publishing. With the transformation of journalism in recent years, some news organizations are lowering the emphasis on editing, though at the expense of copy quality. Hank Glamann, made the following observation about ads for copyeditor positions at newspapers: We want them to be skilled grammarians and wordsmiths and write bright and engaging headlines and must know Quark. But, often, when push comes to shove, we will let every single one of those requirements slide except the last one, because you have to know that in order to push the button at the appointed time.

Traits, Skills, and Training

Besides an excellent command of language, copy editors need broad general knowledge for spotting factual errors, good critical thinking skills in order to recognize inconsistencies, interpersonal skills for dealing with writers and other editors, attention to detail, and a sense of style. Also, they must establish priorities and balance a desire for perfection with the necessity to follow deadlines.

Many copy editors have a college degree, often in journalism, English, or communications. In the United States, copy editing often is taught as a college journalism course, though its name varies. The courses often include news design and pagination.

In the United States, The Dow Jones Newspaper Fund sponsors internships that include two weeks of training. Also, the American Press Institute, the Poynter Institute, the University of North Carolina at Chapel Hill, UC San Diego Extension and conferences of the American Copy Editors Society offer mid-career training for newspaper copy editors and news editors (news copy desk supervisors).

Most newspapers and publishers give copy-editing job candidates an editing test or a tryout. These vary widely and can include general items such as acronyms, current events, math, punctuation, and skills such as the use of Associated Press style, headline writing, infographics editing, and journalism ethics.

In both the U.S. and the U.K., there are no official bodies offering a single recognized qualification. In the U.K., several companies provide a range of courses unofficially recognised within the industry. Training may be on the job or through publishing courses, privately run seminars, and correspondence courses of the Society for Editors and Proofreaders. The National Council for the Training of Journalists also has a qualification for subeditors.

Copyediting Symbols

Copyeditors work to fix the mistakes that writers sometimes miss. They not only watch for continuity problems — those changes in eye color that creep in, or the fact that the brabic plant of Parkinin has leaves on the right side, not the left — but also to fix grammar and punctuation. In the chart below are twenty-two symbols that copyeditors and editors sometimes use to mark manuscripts. These are not the only symbols used, and because they are handwritten, they can vary considerably. Different 'schools' also use slightly different symbols.

Selling to a print house usually means that the author will see a copyedited version of his novel and will have to go through and check each such notation. Learning the symbols and what they mean can help this process move more quickly.

Copyediting is a difficult job, and sometimes the person can overstep the differences between correcting and changing the meaning. Professional writers often have horror stories about bad copyeditors who have changed things for no apparent reason. This often leads to a frantic call to the editor, checking through some of the changes, and deciding what needs to be done. Since books are on a schedule to be produced, it's rare that there's time for another copyediting process, even if it is decided that the original was badly handled.

Copyeditors are professionals, and though there may be occasional problems, they are paid to do the work the publishing houses want. Some work freelance and are hired for specific projects.

Learning to work with copyeditors, and to allow that they probably know their jobs is another key to a successful career in writing.

These symbols are usually written in the margins, sometimes with a short explanation of how the material should be changed.

Insert An Apostrophe	ʼ/
Insert Space	#
Insert Brackets	[/]
Paragraph	¶
Capitalize	Cap
No Paragraph	no¶
Close Up	⁐
Parentheses	(/)
Colon	:/

Period	⊙
Insert Comma	^
Question Mark	?/
Delete	
Quotes	“/”
Delete and Close Up	
Semicolon	;/
Exclamation Point	!/
Spelling	(sp)
Hyphen	=
Transpose	tr
Insert	^
STET (Let it Stand)	Stet

The last symbol — STET — is the writer's friend. It means to leave the original material as the writer intended it, and to ignore the copyeditor's version. However, it should be used with discretion. The copyeditor works for the publishing company, so be aware that some changes may be set to 'house rules.'

■■■

CHAPTER 10

Confusing Words and Common Mistakes in English

English can be confusing. A lot of words are similar but with different meanings. It is almost impossible to avoid making mistakes in English, but you might be able to avoid making these ones.

accept *vs* except

Accept is a verb, which means to agree to take something.

For example: "I always ***accept*** *good advice."*

Except is a preposition or conjunction, which means not including.

For example: "I teach every day ***except*** *Sunday(s)."*

advice *vs* advise

Advice is a noun, which means an opinion that someone offers you about what you should do or how you should act in a particular situation.

For example: "I need someone to give me some ***advice****."*

Advise is a verb, which means to give information and suggest types of action.

*For example: "I **advise** everybody to be nice to their teacher."*

Often in English the noun form ends in ...*ice* and the verb form ends in ...*ise*.

affect vs effect

Affect and ***effect*** are two words that are commonly confused.

affect is usually a verb (action) – **effect** is usually a noun (thing)

Hint: If it's something you're going to do, use "affect." If it's something you've already done, use "effect."

To affect something or someone.

Meaning: To influence, act upon, or change something or someone.

*For example: The noise outside **affected** my performance.*

To have an effect on something or someone.

Note: Effect is followed by the preposition *on* and preceded by an article (*an*, *the*)

Meaning: To have an impact on something or someone.

*For example: His smile had a strange **effect** on me.*

Effect can also mean "the end result".

For example: *The drug has many adverse side **effects**.*

all right *vs* alright

All right has multiple meanings. It can mean ok, acceptable, unhurt.

The single word spelling **alright** has never been accepted as standard.

alone/lonely

Alone, can be used as an adjective or adverb. Either use means without other people or on your own.

*For example: "He likes living **alone**."*

*"I think we're **alone** now." = There are just the two of us here.*

Lonely is an adjective which means you are unhappy because you are not with other people.

*For example: "The house feels **lonely** now that all the children have left home."*

Note – Just because you're alone, doesn't mean you're lonely.

a lot/alot/allot

A lot, meaning a large amount or number of people or things, can be used to modify a noun.

For example: "I need **a lot** of time to develop this web site."

It can also be used as an adverb, meaning very much or very often.

*For example: "I look **a lot** like my sister."*

It has become a common term in speech; and is increasingly used in writing.

Alot does not exist! There is no such word in the English language. If you write it this way – imagine me shouting at you – "No Such Word!"

Allot is a verb, which means to give (especially a share of something) for a particular purpose:

For example: "We were allotted a desk each."

all ready *vs* already

All ready means "completely ready".

For example: "Are you all ready for the test?"

Alreadyis an adverb that means before the present time or earlier than the time expected.

For example: "I asked him to come to the cinema but he'd already seen the film."

Or

"Are you buying Christmas cards already? It's only September!"

altogether *vs* all together

All together (adv) means "together in a single group."

*For example: The waiter asked if we were **all together**.*

Altogether (adv) means "completely" or "in total".

*For example: She wrote less and less often, and eventually she stopped **altogether**.*

any one *vs* anyone

Any one means any single person or thing out of a group of people or things.

*For example:I can recommend **any one** of the books on this site.*

Anyone means any person. It's always written as one word.

*For example:Did **anyone** see that UFO?*

any *vs* some

Any and some are both determiners. They are used to talk about indefinite quantities or numbers, when the exact quantity or number is not important. As a general rule we use **some** for positive statements, and **any** for questions and negative statements.

*For example: I asked the barman if he could get me **some** sparkling* *water. I said, "Excuse me, have you got* ***any*** *sparkling water?" Unfortunately they didn't have* ***any****.*

Note – You will sometimes see **some** in questions and **any** in positive statements. When making an offer, or a request, in order to encourage the person we are speaking to to say "Yes", you can use **some** in a question:

For example: Would you mind fetching ***some*** *gummy bears while you're at the shops?*

You can also use **any** in a positive statement if it comes after a word whose meaning is negative or limiting:

For example:

a) She gave me ***some*** *bad advice.*

b) Really? She rarely gives ***any*** *bad advice.*

apart *vs* a part

Apart (adv) separated by distance or time.

For example: I always feel so lonely when we're apart.

A part (noun) a piece of something that forms the whole of something.

For example: They made me feel like I was a part of the family.

beside *vs* besides

beside is a preposition of place that means at the side of or next to.

For example: The house was beside the Thames.

besides is an adverb or preposition. It means in addition to or also.

For example: Besides water, we carried some fruit. = "In addition to water, we carried some fruit."

bored *vs* boring

bored is an adjective that describes when someone feels tired and unhappy because something is not interesting or because they have nothing to do.

For example: She was so ***bored*** *that she fell asleep.*

boring is an adjective that means something is not interesting or exciting.

For example: The lesson was so ***boring*** *that she fell asleep.*

Note – Most verbs which express emotions, such as *to bore* , may use either the present or the past participle as an adjective, but the meaning of the participles is often different.

borrow *vs* lend

Meaning: To hand out usually for a certain length of time.

Banks *lend* money.

Libraries *lend* books.

For example: *"My mother lent me some money, and I must pay her back soon."*

To borrow:

Meaning: to take with permission usually for a certain length of time.

You can *borrow* money from a bank to buy a house or a car.

You can *borrow* books for up to 4 weeks from libraries in College.

For example: *"I borrowed some money off my mother, and I must pay her back soon."*

bought *vs* brought

bought past tense of the verb **to buy.**

For example: "I bought a newspaper at the newsagents."

brought past tense of the verb **to bring**

For example: "She brought her homework to the lesson."

by *vs* until

Both ***until*** and ***by*** indicate "any time before, but not later than."

Until tells us how long a situation continues. If something happens ***until*** a particular time, you stop doing it at that time.

For example: They lived in a small house ***until*** *September 2003.*

(They stopped living there in September.)

I will be away **until** Wednesday.

(I will be back on Wednesday.)

We also use ***until*** in negative sentences.

For example: Details will ***not*** *be available* ***until*** *January.*

(January is the earliest you can expect to receive the details.)

If something happens ***by*** a particular time, it happens at or before that time. It is often used to indicate a deadline.

For example: You have to finish ***by*** *August 31.*

(August 31 is the last day you can finish; you may finish before this date.)

We also use ***by*** when asking questions.

For example: Will the details be available ***by*** *December?*

(This asks if they will be ready no later than December.)

check (v) *vs* control (v)

To check means to examine. To make certain that something or someone is correct, safe or suitable by examining it or them quickly.

For example: "You should always check your oil, water and tyres before taking your car on a long trip."

To control means to order, limit, instruct or rule something, or someone's actions or behaviour.

For example: "If you can't control your dog, put it on a lead!"

What you shouldn't do is use the verb control in association with people and the work they do.

For example: "I check my students' homework, but I can't control what they do!"

come over (v) *vs* overcome (n)

Come over is a phrasal verb, that can mean several things.

To move from one place to another, or move towards someone.

For example: "Come over here."

To seem to be a particular type of person.

For example: "Politicians often come over as arrogant."

To be influenced suddenly and unexpectedly by a strange feeling.

For example: "Don't stand up too quickly or you may come over dizzy."

Overcome is a verb, which means to defeat or succeed in controlling or dealing with something.

For example: "Using technology can help many people overcome any disabilities they might have."

complement (v) *vs* compliment (n)

Complement is a verb, which means to make something seem better or more attractive when combined.

*For example: "The colours blue and green **complement** each other perfectly."*

Compliment is a noun, which means a remark that expresses approval, admiration or respect.

*For example: "It was the nicest **compliment** anyone had ever paid me."*

If it compl**e**ments something it compl**e**tes it. (With an *e*.)

I like compl***i***ments. (With an *i*.)

concentrate *vs* concentrated

The verb – When you ***concentrate*** you direct all your efforts towards a particular activity, subject or problem.

*For example: You need to **concentrate** harder when you listen to something in another language.*

The adjective – If something is ***concentrated*** it means it has had some liquid removed.

*For example: I prefer freshly squeezed orange juice to **concentrated**.*

council *vs* counsel

Council is a group noun. It refers to a group of people elected or chosen to make decisions or give advice on a particular subject, to represent a particular group of people, or to run a particular organization.

For example: "The local council has decided not to allocate any more funds for the project."

Counsel can be a verb, which means to give advice, especially on social or personal problems.

For example: "She counsels the long-term unemployed on how to get a job."

Counsel can also be a noun, which means advice.

For example: "I should have listened to my father's counsel, and saved some money instead of spending it all."

councillor *vs* counsellor

Councillor is a noun which means an elected member of a local government.

For example: "He was elected to be a councillor in 1998."

Counsellor is a noun, which means someone who is trained to listen to people and give them advice about their problems.

For example: "The student union now employs a counsellor to help students with both personal and work-related problems."

data *vs* datum

This isn't so much a common mistake as a common cause for arguments (as is often the case with words of Latin origin).

The dictionaries treat ***data*** as a group noun, meaning information, especially facts or numbers, collected for examination and consideration and used to help decision-making, or meaning information in an electronic form that can be stored and processed by a computer.

Then they go on to confuse matters by giving the following kind of example:

The ***data was/were*** reviewed before publishing.

So, which is it, ***was*** or ***were***? Strictly speaking '***datum***' is the singular form of and '***data***' is the plural form.

If you're writing for an academic audience, particularly in the sciences, "data" takes a plural verb.

For example: The ***data are*** correct.

But *most* people treat '***data***' as a singular noun, especially when talking about computers etc.

For example: The ***data is*** being transferred from my computer to yours.

decent *vs* descent

Decent is an adjective meaning socially acceptable or good.

For example: Everyone should be entitled to a decent standard of living.

Descent is a noun which can mean a movement downwards, or your ancestry.

For example: The plane began its final descent prior to landing. / "She found out that she was of Welsh descent."

discreet *vs* discrete

Discreet is an adjective.

It means to be careful or modest, not to cause embarrassment or attract too much attention, especially by keeping something secret.

For example: To work for the royal family you have to be very discreet.

Discrete is an adjective.

It means something is distinct and separate or has a clear independent shape or form.

For example: She painted using strong colours, discrete shapes, and rhythmic patterns.

don't have to *vs* mustn't

Don't have to = Do not have to We have to use ***don't have to*** to say that there is no obligation or necessity to do something.

*For example: "You **don't have to** do the exercises at the end of this page."*

Mustn't = must not is a modal verb used to show that something is not allowed. When you use ***mustn't*** you are telling people not to do things. It has the same force as ***don't*** , as in: ***Don't do that!***

*For example: "You **mustn't** drink if you're going to drive."*

downside *vs* underside

Downside is a noun that means the disadvantage of a situation.

*For example: "One of the **downsides** of living in London, of course, is that it is very expensive."*

Underside is a noun that means the side of something that is usually nearest the ground.

*For example: "Look at the **underside** of your iMac display. If you see an Ambient Light Sensor, you have a second generation iMac G5."*

driving test *vs* test drive

A driving test (also known as a driving exam) is a procedure designed to test a person's ability to drive a motor vehicle.

A test drive is when you drive an automobile to assess it, usually before buying it.

e.g *vs* i.e

e.g. stands for *exempli gratia* = for example.

For example: "I like fast cars, e.g. Ferrari and Porche"

In the sentence above you are simply giving an example of the kinds of cars you like – Ferraris and Porches.

i.e. stands for *id est* = that is (in explanation).

For example: "I like fast cars, i.e. any car that can go over 150 mph."

In this second sentence you are giving an explanation of what you consider to be fast.

either *vs* as well/too

Either is used with a negative verb when you are agreeing with something someone doesn't do or like etc.

For example: *B agrees with A in the negative*

A - "I don't like cheese." B - "I don't like it ***either****."*

A- "I haven't seen Lord of the Rings." B - "I haven't seen it ***either****."*

As well / Too are used with an affirmative verb when you are agreeing with something someone does or likes etc.

For example: B agrees with A in the positive

A - "I love ice cream." B - "I love it ***too****." / "I love it* ***as well****."*

A- "I've seen Gladiator." B – "I've seen it ***too****." / "I've seen it* ***as well****."*

every day *vs* everyday

Every day – Here every is a determiner and day is a noun.

When you say every day you mean each day without exception.

For example: You have been late for school every day this week.

Everyday is an adjective.

When you say everyday you mean ordinary, unremarkable.

For example: My culture pages offer an insight into the everyday life of Britain.

excited *vs* exciting

Excited is an adjective that describes when someone feels happy and enthusiastic about something.

*For example: She was so **excited** that she couldn't sleep.*

Exciting is an adjective that means something is making you excited.

*For example: The football match was so **exciting** that she couldn't wait to tell everyone about it.*

expand *vs* expend

Expand is a transitive or intransitive verb. It means to increase in size, number or importance, or to make something increase.

For example: Jarp is expanding his vocabulary on the forum, but Hermine's hips are expanding as well.

Expend is a transitive verb. It means to use or spend something (especially time, effort or money).

For example: She is expending a lot of effort to help her students.

experience *vs* experience(s)

Experience can be an uncountable noun. You use it when you're talking about knowledge or skill which is obtained from doing, seeing or feeling things.

For example: Do you have any experience of working internationally?

Experience(s) can be a countable noun. You use it when you are talking about a particular incident or incidents that affect you.

For example: It was interesting hearing about his experiences during the war.

Experience can also be a verb. It means something that happens to you, or something you feel.

For example: When I first moved to Germany I experienced a lot of problems.

fewer *vs* less

Everyone gets this wrong – including native speakers. The general rule is to use **fewer** for things you can count (individually), and **less** for things you can only measure.

For example: There were fewer days below freezing last winter. (Days can be counted.)

I drink less coffee than she does. (Coffee cannot be counted individually it has to be measured).

Note – "Less" has to do with how much. "Fewer" has to do with how many.

for *vs* since

The prepositions ***for*** and ***since*** are often used with time expressions.

For indicates a period of time.

*For example: I have been working here **for** 2 years.*

Since indicates a point in time.

*For example: I have been working here **since** the year before last.*

good *vs* well

Good is an adjective. We use good when we want to give more information about a noun.

*For example: My dog Sam is very **good**.* He's a ***good*** dog.

*She didn't speak very **good** English.* Her English isn't very ***good***.

Well is usually used as an adverb. We use well when we want to give more information about a verb.

*For example: He usually behaves very **well**.*

*She didn't speak English very **well**.*

Note – The exception to this can be when you talk about someone's health:

*For example: She wasn't a **well** woman.*

and when you describe sensations:

*For example: This pizza tastes/smells/ looks **good**.*

If you say "You look ***good***." It means they look attractive.

If you say "You look ***well***." It means they look healthy.

hard *vs* hardly

Hard is an adjective. It can mean solid, industrious, or difficult.

*For example: Heating the clay makes it **hard*** (solid).

*She is a **hard*** (industrious) *worker.*

*It was a **hard*** (difficult) *test.*

Hardly is an adverb and means only just or certainly not.

*For example: The teacher spoke so quietly I could **hardly*** (only just) *hear her.*

You can **hardly** *(certainly not)* expect me to do the test for you!

hear *vs* listen

hear is a verb that means to receive or become aware of a sound using your ears, so you don't have to make an effort in order to just hear something.

*For example: She **heard** a noise outside.*

listen is a verb that means to give attention to someone or something in order to hear them, so you make an make an effort in order to hear something properly.

*For example: She **listened** to the noise and realised it was only a cat.*

Note– In some circumstances we use hear when we listen to someone or something attentively or officially.

*For example: I **heard** a really interesting speech on the radio this morning.*

*These people need to be **heard**.*

heroin *vs* heroine

Heroin is a noun, it is a powerful illegal drug, obtained from morphine and is extremely addictive.

For example: "He was arrested for supplying heroin, a class A drug."

Heroine is a female person who is admired for having done something very brave or having achieved something great. The male equivalent is hero.

For example: "Grace Darling is one of England's best known heroines."

he's *vs* his

He's is the short form of 'he is' or 'he has'.

*For example: " Don't be scared – **he's** very friendly."*

His is a possesive pronoun, it is used to show something belonging to or connected with a man, boy or male animal that has just been mentioned.

*For example: "Mark just phoned to say he'd left his coat behind. Do you know if this is **his**?"*

holiday *vs* weekend

A holiday (noun), a time, often one or two weeks, when someone does not go to work or school but is free to do what they want, such as travel or relax. You usually have to book your holiday with your boss.

For example: "Where are you going on holiday this year? Somewhere nice I hope."

The weekend (noun) – The time from Saturday and Sunday, or Friday evening until Sunday night. It's the part of the week in which most paid workers living in the West do not go to work. It is a time for leisure and recreation, and/or for religious activities. ...

For example: "What are you doing this weekend? Anything nice?"

homework *vs* housework

Homework (noun) – It refers to tasks assigned to students by teachers to be completed mostly outside of class, and derives its name from the fact that most students do the majority of such work at home.

For example: "A lot of students in the UK get too much homework."

Housework (noun) – It refers to domestic household chores such as cleaning and cooking.

For example: "I never seem to have enough time to do the housework. There's always something that needs dusting or polishing."

"How do you do?" *vs* "How are you?"

If I had a Euro for every time someone got this one wrong – I'd be a rich bunny!

How do you do?

This **is not** a question. It is another, very formal way of saying **"Hello."** It is also very British.

The correct response is; "Pleased to meet you." or "How do you do." or just "Hello."

We only really use it the **first time** we meet someone.

How are you?

This **is** a question.

A polite response is; "I'm fine thanks. And you?"

I *vs* me

Usually we choose the correct form by instinct.

*For example: **I** am a teacher. (not **me**)*

*Give that to **me**. (not **I**)*

There are other times when people make mistakes with these two pronouns. **I/me** is difficult when it is coupled with another pronoun or with a noun. This is when you have to think about the subject/object in a sentence.

*For example: "It was **I** who did the homework," or "It was **me** who did the homework."*

Make the statement simpler:

"**I** did the homework." so "It was **I** who did the homework," is correct.

The teacher gave the homework to my friend and **me**. (Not **I**)

interested *vs* interesting

Interested is a past participle. When used as an adjective it says how someone feels.

*For example: "I was very **interested** in the lesson".*

Interesting is a present participle. When used as an adjective it describes the people or things that cause the feelings.

*For example: "It was an **interesting** lesson."*

lay *vs* lie

Lay is an irregular transitive verb (lay / laid/ laid – laying). It needs a direct object. It means to put something or someone down (often in a horizontal postion).

For example: "Lay your head on the pillow."

Lie is an irregular intransitive verb (lie / lay / lain – lying). It does not take a direct object. It means to rest in a horizontal position or to be located somewhere.

For example: "If you are tired lie here and have a rest."

"Nottingham lies in the Midlands."

lay down *vs* lie down

Lay down has several different meanings.

If you lay something down it can mean you officially establish a rule, or officially state the way in which something should be done.

For example: Please follow the rules laid down by the administrator.

If you lay something down your weapons it means you stop fighting.

For example: They laid down their guns and surrendered.

If you lay wine down it means you are storing it for drinking in the future.

For example: I laid down this bottle in 1998, it should be perfect for drinking now.

Lie down means to move into a position in which your body is flat, usually in order to sleep or rest.

For example: "If you are tired lie down and have a rest."

look at *vs* watch

In this context ***look*** is usually followed by the preposition ***at***.

When you ***look at*** someone or something you are interested in the appearance.

Generally we ***look at*** things that are static.

For example: Look at these photos, they're really good.

I went to the art gallery to look at the exhibition of paintings.

Watch is a verb.

When you ***watch*** someone or something you are interested in what happens.

Generally we ***watch*** things that move or change state.

For example: I watch TV every night.

The security guard watched the shoplifter steal the clock.

■■■

Chapter 11

Editing Samples

Sample 1

Original

Many of my high school teachers had only a certain amount of time to focus on certain aspects of a particular subject that they were teaching their students. They could not spend a longer period on a certain section even if it was of interest to them or the students.

They often complained that they were unable to spend a long time on an issue that was of interest to the students because they were required to teach students a certain amount of subsections or issues of a particular subject in order to specialize them in that subject as a whole. Teachers willingly comply with the directives that superiors issue because of the loyalty those teachers as subordinates have for their immediate superior the principal.

This is the reason teachers do not or are not willing to stray from the regulations or directives superimposed on them.

Edited

Many of my high-school teachers had only limited time to focus on subjects to be taught. As a result, they often complained of being unable to spend sufficient time on an issue of interest to the students, because they were required to teach a set number of subsections of a particular subject in order for students to specialize in that subject as a whole. Yet teachers, even while harbouring such dissatisfaction, willingly comply with the directives that superiors issue because of the loyalty they as subordinates have to their immediate superior, the principal. Thus, teachers either do not or are not willing to stray from the regulations or directives superimposed on them.

Sample 2

Original

There are many reasons why I want to do work in this field. One very important reason is the prevalence of language and speech disorders among children and adults. I want to contribute and help these children and adults so they can become better effective communicators. Communication is an important and vital need in our society. Because of severe speech problems, some people may be unable to use the traditional communication channels. This is what drives me to enter into a field that can effectively help people modify and alter their communication abilities. Speech Language Pathologist have helped to prevent, identify, evaluate, treat, and rehabilitate communication disorders across the entire spectrum. Another reason I am intrigued, is by the diversity of the field. Who could become board in this field with all the possibilities? There are so many different avenues that can be explored, for example aphasia, oral motor disorders or language disorders. One of the main reasons I am drawn to your programme is the fact that you allow your students to explore all paths of this field. So far I have had most of my clinical experience working with pre-school children but I am excited to work with older children and adults. The etiologies of the disorders are also very interesting. There are so many things that are unknown, which allows room for so much research.

Edited

My most important reason for choosing a career in speech language pathology is the prevalence of language and speech disorders among children and adults. Because of severe speech problems, many people may be unable to use the traditional communication channels that are vital tools in our society. Wanting to contribute by helping these children and adults become more effective communicators, I am attracted to a field directed at preventing, identifying, evaluating, treating, and rehabilitating communication disorders across the entire spectrum. I am also intrigued by the diversity of the field, by the many different avenues to be explored, including aphasia, oral motor disorders, or language disorders. A major reason I am drawn to your program is that you allow your students to explore all these paths. The etiologies of the disorders also interest me greatly. The many things still unknown allow room for tremendous research.

Sample 3

Original

Ramesh suggests several reasons why the capitalism should be destroyed. His views on economic factors in that period have been recognized as great ones and have affected a lot on the current economics. However, apparently his predictions on the collapse of capitalism and appearance of socialism do not happen. Oppositely, in these days, socialism has broken down. In addition, there are many errors that have founded on his theory that does not match with this days like three arguments aforementioned. Nevertheless, the fact that how exactly he pointed out problems of capitalism which has appeared with getting attentions for 50 years is really remarkable.

Edited

Ramesh suggests several reasons why capitalism should be destroyed, and his views on economic factors, ideas that have greatly affected current economics, have been recognized as great ones for his time. However, apparently his predictions on the collapse of capitalism and appearance of socialism have not come to pass. On the contrary, today it is socialism that has broken down. In addition, his theory proposes many erroneous assumptions, like the three arguments aforementioned, that are contrary to current situations. Nevertheless, that he exactly pointed out problems of capitalism that have appeared and commanded attention for 50 years is really remarkable.

Sample 4

Original

My biology high school teacher has a wonderful personality. She was close to the student and at the same time has her respect as a teacher. She has a quite personality, which allows all the student to talk and ask when ever they want. When she was explaining some subject, she was always trying to make it simple and acceptable to understand. She is the kind of people who understand others circumstances for example, if some of the students could not attend the quiz she will listen to the reasons that kept the student for not attending the quiz and she gave her another chance. She was so corporative with all the students. Academically, she was so versed in her specialty. She has a strong self confident and that make her more strong and expert in her subject.

Edited

My high-school biology teacher had a wonderful personality. She was close to the students but at the same time was respected as a teacher. A quiet person who allowed students to talk and ask questions whenever they wanted, when she explained material, she always tried to make it simple and easily understandable. She was also the kind of person who understands the circumstances of others; for example, if a student could not attend a quiz, she would listen to the reasons why then give her a chance to make it up. She cooperated in this way equally with all the students. Academically, she was so well versed in her specialty that she was extremely self-confident, which in turn made her even stronger and more expert in her subject.

Sample 5

Original

Most customers experience the attribution process relating to purchase. Customers can work much more attribution process with regard to purchase on online, rather than on offline because customers on online cannot use the best their senses-look, taste, feel, smell, and sound. They just use their experiences, brand, advertising, word-of-mouth. The negative attribution on satisfaction shows the minus (-) impact to repurchase intention. Thus, manager should tract continuous the customer responses after customer bought. This might provide feedback to company and help customer enhance positively the perception by the negative attribution. It is based on constant development of the Internet technologies. Both tracking effective customer and building database can impact to the company's long-term development.

Edited

Most customers experience the attribution process related to purchase. With regard to purchases online rather than offline, such attribution processes are more focused because customers online cannot use their senses—look, taste, feel, smell, and sound. They simply draw upon their experiences, brand name, advertising, and word-of-mouth. A negative attribution on satisfaction shows the minus (–) impact on repurchase intention.

Thus, managers should continuously track customer responses after customer purchase. Such follow-up might provide feedback to the company and help them enhance positive customer perception to counteract negative attribution. Even though tracking requires constant development of Internet technologies, both effective customer tracking and the building of a database can positively impact the company's long-term development.

Essay Editing

Sample

The theory I have chosen to evaluate is that of Dr. Elisabeth Kubler–Ross and her five stages theory of dying leading to the Grief Curve. (1969). I have decided to do this as I have used a adaptation of this in some of the work I do with groups in looking at how they as leaders manage change for themselves and others, when facing changes at work – the "change curve".

The stages of the change curve resemble very closely those of Kubler–Ross's grief curve.

I became aware, that not only was the original research completed by Kubler–Ross being questioned, (Gorle 2002) Fitchett (1980) (Chaban 1999), but work undertaken by others (Dunphy and Stace (1988), Bridges (1995) and Senge (1999) were all putting forward their own ideas, assumptions and understandings of organizational change which conflicted with hers.

Why has the theory from Kubler-Ross and later adapted to apply as a tool to help individuals to manage change been so popular until recently? In my opinion, the strength of the theory may be in its apparent simplicity. Dr Kubler- Ross presented 5 stages that a terminally ill person may go through in trying to cope with this news.

She categorised these 5 stages as denial, anger, bargaining, depression and acceptance. Whilst she may not have explicitly stated that a person needed to go through all 5 stages in sequence, this is how it has been interpreted by many. This has further been changed over the years by many, including doctors, nurses, and other health care professionals into the 5 stages of Grief.

The change curve (based on Kubler-Ross's work) and used by some consultants (including the author) states that individuals facing change may go through some or all of the following stages: shock, retreat, self–doubt, apathy, resolve, taking stock and new goals.

The stages of the curve represent the stages people may go through or become stuck at when change occurs, whether that change is positive or negative. The curve is applicable to change that is acceptable and welcomed or unacceptable and imposed, although the latter will probably be more difficult to manage.

John Fisher (1999) also supports this work further with his personal transition curve, outlining how individuals deal with personal change. The phases of this curve are anxiety, happiness, fear, threat, guilt, depression, disillusionment (this stage was added in 2003), hostility and denial. He argues that any change no matter how small, has the potential to impact on an individual and may generate conflict between their existing and anticipated changed values and beliefs.

Fisher, with Dr. David Savage (1999) wrote about personal construct psychology theory, building on the work of George Kelly (1955), which proposed "we must understand how the other person sees their world and what meaning they attribute to things in order to effectively communicate and connect with them" This theory views that people have the power to change and grow and are only limited by the vision they have of themselves and by their own internal "blinkers" that might prevent future development.

All of the above have stages or phases that people can begin to put a name to and justify their feelings. In my opinion, people like to put themselves into a box and create meaning. For example, (Honey and Mumford's learning styles inventory (1982), Belbin's team roles (1981), Blanchard's situational leadership model (1969). It is not the author's view that this is correct or to be encouraged. However, people like to know more about themselves and try to find out why they are thinking, feeling, behaving as they are. Total experience for 20 years as firstly an employed trainer within the public sector and then a consultant working in both large and small organizations throughout the UK shows that this may be so. In managing others it can help to start to formulate a plan to help them through one stage and onto the next. I am not suggesting it will always be easy but it is easy to understand.

However, is it's weakness in its simplicity? The work that Kubler Ross completed in the 1960's and 1970's has been questioned as none of her research has been published, there is no explicit empirical base, and the number of patients used was relatively low to base predictions upon. Some patients did not know that they were dying and/or being used for research. It is also alleged by Chaban, (1991) whilst doing some research for her PhD Thesis on Kubler–Ross that Kubler–Ross had had access to the work of many others, including two books by Glaser and Strauss (1965 and 1968) which bore similarities to her subsequent book, On Death and Dying (1969).

Heather Robertson, writing in the Elm Street Magazine in September 1999 writes of her disappointment when she discovered that Kubler-Ross's research "seemed to be derived from rambling conversations with anonymous patients at the University of Chicago's Billings Hospital" She goes on to describe how the book contained only parts of these interviews and that the work is difficult to verify because of Kubler-Ross's practise of using either first names or pseudonyms with no dates. Whilst this might seem to be protecting confidentiality, this would also be in conflict with Kubler-Ross' practice of interviewing patients, sometimes on television, without them and/or their families knowing they were dying. So, in my opinion, there are some questionable ethical issues to be considered. In fact, Chaban goes onto to suggest that Carl Nighswonger, a Billings Hospital chaplain who jointly interviewed patients with Kubler-Ross and was a professor at in the University of Chicago Divinity School, was in fact responsible for the theory. Kubler-Ross appears to reduce all personal experiences to predictable universal stages.

Edited

The theory I have chosen to evaluate is that of Dr. Elisabeth Kubler-Ross and her theory of the five stages of dying leading to the Grief Curve (1969). I selected this theory because I used an adaptation of it in some of my previous work; I met with groups to determine how they, as leaders, manage change for themselves and others when they faced changes at work – the "change curve".

The stages of the change curve very closely resemble the ones presented by Kubler-Ross and her grief curve. I became aware that the original research completed by Kubler-Ross was being questioned by Gorle (2002), Fitchett (1980) and Chaban (1999). Work was also undertaken by others such as Dunphy and Stace (1988), Bridges (1995) and Senge (1999). They all put forward their own ideas, assumptions and understandings of organisational change which conflicted with those of Kubler-Ross.

Why has the theory from Kubler-Ross which was later adapted as a tool to help individuals manage change become so popular recently? In my opinion, the strength of the theory may lie in its apparent simplicity. Dr. Kubler-Ross presented 5 stages that a terminally ill person often expereinces when attempting to cope with this news. She categorised these 5 stages as denial, anger, bargaining, depression and acceptance. Although she never explicitly stated that a person needed to experience all 5 stages in sequence, many others have interpreted her theory this way. Many health care professionals including doctors and nurses have further revised this theory over the years into the 5 stages of grief.

The change curve is based on the work of Kubler–Ross, and is used by certain consultants including the author. This theory states that individuals facing change may progress through some or all of the following stages:

- Shock
- Retreat
- Self-Doubt
- Apathy
- Resolve
- Taking Stock

The stages of the curve represent each of the stages people may go through or become stuck at when change occurs, regardless of whether the change is positive or negative; the curve is applicable to both change that is acceptable and welcomed or unacceptable and imposed. However, the latter is generally acknowledged as more difficult to manage.

John Fisher (1999) further supports this work with his personal transition curve which outlines how individuals deal with personal change. The phases of this curve include: anxiety, happiness, fear, threat, guilt, depression, disillusionment (this stage was added in 2003), hostility and denial. He argues that any change, no matter how small, has the potential to impact an individual. It may also generate conflict between existing and anticipated values and beliefs.

Fisher and Dr. David Savage (1999) wrote about personal construct psychology theory. They built on the work of George Kelly (1955) which proposed that "we must understand how the other person sees their world and what meaning they attribute to things in order to effectively communicate and connect with them". This theory claims that people have the power to change and grow; they are only limited by their own vision of themselves and by their internal "blinkers" that may prevent future development.

All of the above have stages or phases that people can begin to identify in order to justify their feelings. In my opinion, people like to place themselves into a box and create meaning. For example, Honey and Mumford's learning styles inventory (1982), Belbin's team roles (1981) and Blanchard's situational leadership model (1969). that the author does not claim that this is correct or should be encouraged. However, people like to discover more about themselves and try to determine why they are thinking, feeling or behaving a certain way.

Twenty years of experience working as an employed trainer within the public sector and as a consultant in large and small organisations throughout the UK reveals that this may indeed be the case. In regards to managing others, it may prove helpful to begin formulating a plan to help them through one stage and onto the next. I am not suggesting it will always be easy, but it is easy to understand.

However, does the weakness of Kubler-Ross' theory lie in its simplicity? The work that Kubler-Ross completed in the 1960s and 1970s has been questioned for numerous reasons. None of her research has been published, no explicit empirical base exists, and the number of patients used was relatively low to formulate accurate predictions. In addition, some patients did not realize they were dying and/or being studied for research purposes. While conducting research for her Ph.D. thesis on Kubler-Ross, Chaban (1991) also alleged that Kubler-Ross had had access to the work of many others. This included two books by Glaser and Strauss (1965 and 1968) which bore similarities to her subsequent book, *On Death and Dying* (1969).

In the September 1999 edition of the *Elm Street Magazine*, Heather Robertson expressed her disappointment when she discovered that the research of Kubler-Ross "seemed to be derived from rambling conversations with anonymous patients at the University of Chicago's Billings Hospital". She went on to describe how the book contained only partial interviews and that the work was difficult to verify because of Kubler-Ross practise of using first names or pseudonyms with no dates. She may have wantd to protect the confidentiality of the patients,. However, this is in conflict with her practice of interviewing patients, sometimes on television, without them and/or their families knowing they were dying. Consequently, in my opinion, some questionable ethical issues must be seriously considered. In fact, Chaban goes on to suggest that Carl Nighswonger, a professor at the University of Chicago Divinity School and a Billings Hospital chaplain who jointly interviewed patients with Kubler-Ross was actually responsible for the theory. Kubler-Ross appears to reduce all personal experiences to predictable universal stages.

Novel Editing

Unedited Version of Historical Novel, *River of Reckoning*

By the time our otherwise pleasant visit with the grandparents ended, I had made my decision. The railroad life with its perfect schedules imposing order on society, and with its tracks knitting the trans-Mississippi West into a quilt work stitched together with crossties, and with its massive corporate structure that reinvented the style of overseers and serfs, it could not be the life for me. After considering retiring, or opening a locomotive factory to build big steam engines, or becoming a cattle man like Big George, or just moving my whole family to California for the hell of it, I decided to stay a steamboat man, to run my boats one step ahead of Old Nick–as I named the railroads–by emphasizing our operation on the Upper Missouri River. Unless the Northern route was chosen by Washington, D.C. to be the transcontinental railroad, I would be an old man before rail pierced that part of America. My decision came to me while I played my violin to an Ohio River sunset, when the river bends red and gold across a darkening land.

At that moment I heard the unmistakable hoot from a Big Cat steamboat, and when my steamboat came into view, I knew I had led a charmed life, to be so favored by the gods that I had been allowed to experience such a sublime joy. She was our newest steamboat, named *Saber Tooth Tiger* after the bones farmers were finding in dry washes in Dakota Territory. According to Rachel, museum men from the East had also found elephant skeletons with huge, curving tusks in Dakota Territory sands.

***

Before cock's crow, I woke to the clatter of a carriage halting at our front door, followed by the sharp rapping of a metal cane on our door. When mother opened the peep-hole, she giggled and said, "I'm glad you're back early."

From my shadowed perch, I shuddered at the large man's hulking figure, he dressed in a rich fur coat and hunter's hat, a holster straining to surround the handgun strapped to his right thigh, a scabbard and war sword dangling on his left hip. His furs made a swishing sound when he bent to meet my mother's long, lingering kiss.

"I have a surprise for you," she told him. "It's David! Duke Paul sent him home."

The big man turned, to my horror indeed Prince Sigmund, and fixed angry eyes on me.”You? I don’t believe it!”

“Duke Paul sent me home at Rotterdam.”

“Really? Who came with you?” he asked, piercing me with his gaze.

“No one.”

“Hard to believe,” he growled.

“I swear it.”

“Damn unlikely.” He seemed to see right through me. “I told Duke Paul to be sure you reached America.”

Mother bristled at his tone. ”He is of my flesh and blood, your highness. Please welcome him to your domains.”

“Mine while my brother stays abroad.” He turned back to me. “My attendants will return you to the workers,” chambers, to the single men’s quarters. Time will tell if you have lied to me, Jew Boy.” I did not like the threatening tone in his voice, with its hints of his sadistic nature, his foremost trait which staff nannies claimed first became discernible as a child, when Duke Sigmund laughed while methodically ripping wings from birds he trapped in nets. Deathly pale, my mother frowned at him while she helped me gather my things and hugged me as Prince Sigmund’s footman reminded me which road to walk.’

Edited Version of Historical Novel, *River of Reckoning*

While we visited with Solomon’s grandparents, and I had time and leisure on my hands, I thought about my options. I considered retiring. I considered opening a locomotive factory to build big steam engines. I considered becoming a cattle man like Big George. I thought about moving my whole family to California and looking for new enterprises. I kept on thinking about these possibilities on the journey back home, and for the first few days back at *Richter Haus*.

I pondered all the options one evening as I played my violin to an Ohio River sunset. The river bends glowed like a red and gold ribbon winding across the darkening land. Suddenly, I heard the unmistakable hoot from a Big Cat steamboat. Then the boat herself hove into sight. She was our newest steamboat, named *Saber Tooth Tiger* after the bones farmers were finding in dry washes in Dakota Territory. According to Rachel, museum men from the East had also found elephant skeletons with huge, curving tusks in the sands of the Dakota Territory. When I saw the ship, I knew that I had been favored by the gods in being allowed to experience so many sublime joys.

I knew at that moment that I would remain a steamboat man and not become a railroad man. The railroad life, with its perfect schedules imposing order on society, and with its tracks knitting the trans-Mississippi West into a quiltwork stitched together with cross-ties, with its massive corporate structure reinventing the roles of overseers and serfs – this could not be the life for me.

As I gazed at the final rays of the sun, the solution leapt into my mind. I would run my boats one step ahead of "Old Nick" - as I named the railroads - by emphasizing Big Cat's operation on the Upper Missouri River. Unless the Northern route were chosen by Washington, D.C. for the transcontinental railroad, I would be an old man before rail pierced that part of America.

Two days later, before cock's crow, I woke to the clatter of a carriage halting at our front door, followed by the sharp rapping of a metal cane on our door. When mother opened the peep-hole, she giggled and said, "I'm glad you're back early. Give me a minute to get ready."

We discarded our night-shirts and threw on our clothes in scant seconds. I sat in the shadows near the bed, as a large man's figure, dressed in a rich fur coat and beaver hat, hulked into the room. A holstered handgun nestled against his right thigh, and on his left hip dangled a war sword in its scabbard. Prince Sigmund himself seemed to me much more menacing than either weapon. His furs made a swishing sound when he bent to meet my mother's long, lingering kiss.

She broke away. "I have a surprise for you," she told him. "It's David! Duke Paul sent him home."

The big man turned, and fixed angry eyes on me. "You? I don't believe it!"

"Duke Paul sent me home at Rotterdam," I lied.

"Really? Who came with you?"

"No one."

"Hard to believe," he growled."

"I swear it."

"Damn unlikely." He seemed to see right through me. "I told Duke Paul to be sure you reached America." Suddenly I understood why Duke Paul had uncharacteristically cut my protests short, and insisted on me accompanying him to America. Duke Sigmund had wanted me out of the way so that he could pursue his dalliance. My blood ran hot, then cold at the realization.

Mother bristled at the Duke's tone. "He is of my flesh and blood, your highness. Please welcome him to your domain."

"Mine while my brother stays abroad," he said, then turned back to me. "My attendants will return you to the workers' chambers, to the single men's quarters. Time will tell if you have lied to me, Jew Boy." I did not like the threatening tone in his voice. I remembered a story told by one of the castle nannies, who said that young Sigmund used to trap birds in nets, then rip off their wings, laughing as he killed. A heavy silence hung in the air while mother and I gathered my things. She hugged me, said a quick goodbye, then, accompanied by, or guarded by (I could not tell which) one of the Duke's footmen, I left.

■■■

Other Books on

WORD POWER SERIES

27.	School Essays & Letters for Juniors	75/-
28.	Common Mistakes in English	95/-
29.	The Power of Writing	150/-
30.	Learn English in 21 Lessons	95/-
31.	First English Dictionary	95/-
32.	Boost Your Spelling Power	95/-
33.	Self-Help to English Conversation	95/-
34.	The Art of Effective Communication	110/-
35.	A Book of Proverbs & Quotations	95/-
36.	Word Power Made Easy	95/-
37.	English Grammar :Easier Way	125/-
38.	General English for Competitive Examinations	125/-
39.	Spoken English	95/-
40.	School Essays, Letters and Phrases	95/-
41.	How to Write & Speak Better English	95/-
42.	Quote Unquote (A Handbook of Famous Quotations)	125/-
43.	Improve Your Vocabulary	125/-
44.	Common Errors in English	95/-
45.	The Art of Effective Letter Writing	95/-
46.	Synonyms & Antonyms	95/
47.	Idioms	95/-
48.	Business Letters	95/-

Unit No. 220, 2nd Floor, 4735/22,
Prakash Deep Building,Ansari Road, Darya Ganj,
New Delhi- 110002, Ph.: 32903912, 23280047
• E-mail : lotus_press@sify.com, www.lotuspress.co.in